Leadership Succession and Transition for Museums and Arts Organizations

American Alliance of Museums

The American Alliance of Museums has been bringing museums together since 1906, helping to develop standards and best practices, gathering and sharing knowledge, and providing advocacy on issues of concern to the entire museum community. Representing more than thirty-five thousand individual museum professionals and volunteers, institutions, and corporate partners serving the museum field, the Alliance stands for the broad scope of the museum community.

The American Alliance of Museums' mission is to champion museums and nurture excellence in partnership with its members and allies.

Books published by AAM further the Alliance's mission to make standards and best practices for the broad museum community widely available.

Leadership Succession and Transition for Museums and Arts Organizations

A Guide for Boards and Chief Executives

Kaywin Feldman

ROWMAN & LITTLEFIELD
Lanham • Boulder • New York • London

To my father, Donald Alexander Feldman, who taught me everything important.

Published by Rowman & Littlefield
An imprint of The Rowman & Littlefield Publishing Group, Inc.
4501 Forbes Boulevard, Suite 200, Lanham, Maryland 20706
www.rowman.com

86-90 Paul Street, London EC2A 4NE

British Library Cataloguing in Publication Information Available

Library of Congress Cataloging-in-Publication Data Available

ISBN 978-1-5381-8562-9 (cloth: alk. paper)
ISBN 978-1-5381-8563-6 (pbk.: alk. paper)
ISBN 978-1-5381-8564-3 (electronic)

♾™ The paper used in this publication meets the minimum requirements of American National Standard for Information Sciences—Permanence of Paper for Printed Library Materials, ANSI/NISO Z39.48-1992.

Contents

Introduction: Leadership Succession and Transition for Museums
and Arts Organizations: A Guide for Boards and Chief Executives   vii

1   Succession Planning   1

2   The Departure   11

3   The Search   21

4   The Selection   33

5   The Leader   43

6   The Bias Traps   57

7   The First Six Months   71

8   The Next Six to Twelve Months: Strap In!   89

9   The First-Time CEO and the Internal Candidate   103

10   The Dream Job   113

Appendix: A Menu of My Favorite Interview Questions
(compiled over a decade)   119

Acknowledgments   127

Bibliography   129

Index   139

About the Author   149

Introduction: Leadership Succession and Transition for Museums and Arts Organizations: A Guide for Boards and Chief Executives

> In the middle of the journey of our life I came to myself within a dark wood where the straight way was lost. Ah, how hard a thing it is to tell what a wild, and rough, and stubborn wood this was, which in my thought renews the fear!
> —Dante Alighieri, *The Divine Comedy*[1]

The opening phrase of Dante's *Divine Comedy* grabs the reader immediately; who of us hasn't fearfully navigated a metaphorical dark wood where the path forward is unclear? Those moments are filled with ambiguity and uncertainty, made more challenging by the potential consequences of bad choices.

Life is filled with transitions, both personal and professional, many of which we have little direct control over. The most frightening transitions are the ones without a plan or a playbook. Although Dante's journey was a spiritual one, it is nonetheless a good metaphor for the transformation that happens to organizations and chief executives during the period of a leadership change. Like the *Divine Comedy*, these passages involve multiple distinct phases and offer a challenging journey of self-awareness, growth, and opportunity for individuals and institutions.

At the age of thirty-one, after serving as a museum director for four years in Fresno, California, I was offered the job of leading the Memphis Brooks Museum of Art. I found out that I was the second-choice candidate after the lead candidate declined the opportunity, which didn't feel very good. I drove around Fresno for a week with the draft contract in the back seat of my car, visible from the rearview mirror during my reluctant glances back there. I was suffering from the common condition of cold feet. Was this the right move for me? Did they really believe in me in Memphis? Was I ready to leave all that we had created in Fresno? Would I be letting a lot of people down, people who had taken a chance on me and invested in my leadership? One day, the song

"Walking in Memphis" by Marc Cohn came on the car radio, and I suddenly knew this was indeed my next path through the woods. I signed the contract an hour later. Sometimes we just need a push to take the transition plunge, even if it is just from a pop song playing on the radio! Working in Memphis was one of my greatest life privileges, and I will forever be grateful to Marc Cohn for pushing me over the line of fear and anxiety.

The interview process, the decision to leave Fresno and subsequent departure, followed by arrival and onboarding in Memphis, were all different phases of transition both for me and for all the museums I would eventually serve. I have experienced this journey four times in my life, and while I understand the transition process much better, the emotions still run high, and the opportunities for missteps for leaders, trustees, and stakeholders abound.

TAKEOFF AND LANDING

It is estimated that approximately 90 percent of airline accidents occur during the taxi, takeoff, and landing phases of airplane travel. David L. Baker has advised, "Flying is so many parts skill, so many parts planning, so many parts maintenance, and so many parts luck. The trick is to reduce the luck by increasing the others."[2] As I have approached my leadership transitions, contemplating how to leave one museum and begin at another, my husband always reminds me that most airline mishaps occur at takeoff and landing, emphasizing the need to approach each stage thoughtfully, carefully, and with a plan. Don't leave your transition to luck.

> Whether successful or not, all the experienced leaders we spoke to agreed that their transitions into new companies . . . were more difficult than anything they had experienced in their careers. —Dan Ciampa and Michael Watkins, *Right from the Start: Taking Charge in a New Leadership Role*[3]

Nonprofit leaders and institutions are at their most vulnerable during times of transition, and it is critical that executive leaders, staff, stakeholders, and volunteer leadership succeed in this difficult phase. Surprisingly, staff and boards often invent the practice anew each time there is a transition. Given that most board terms are around three years (usually renewable two or three times) and the average tenure for a nonprofit leader is seven to eight years, it is common that each change of leadership is navigated by a board of trustees who are likely new to the organization and may have never managed a leadership transition there.[4] And only a few of them might have served on search committees of other nonprofit boards. They are literally learning on the job each time a director leaves. Few new corporate leaders feel they were adequately supported by the board and institution after they begin their new role.[5]

After serving as a museum director for thirty years, I am struck by the difficulty museum boards have in replacing the CEO. I have interviewed for several museum director roles, and I have served on the boards of over a dozen nonprofits, chairing two of them and leading two CEO searches. I have frequently sat on both sides of the CEO hiring table, as a candidate and as a trustee. Few nonprofit trustees have experience hiring leaders, and they flounder when confronted with the challenge. On several occasions, I have watched successful business leaders botch interviews because they are not sure how to hire a nonprofit CEO and they don't really know much about the business of the nonprofit. Sometimes, I fear, it is due to their assumption that running a nonprofit is not very difficult, leading to decisions they would never make in their own companies. Without a road map, proper planning, and guidance, they often default to hiring for chemistry alone. While chemistry is extremely important, the proper leadership qualities for the moment in the organization's history are even more essential.

I decided that someone needs to write a useful primer on nonprofit leadership transition, and that person might as well be me. As Stephen Covey has taught us, the main thing is keeping the main thing, the main thing.[6] And the main thing is finding a skilled leader who matches the culture and ambition of the organization in an increasingly complex world and then setting that leader on a path to succeed.

LIMINALITY

Liminality (from the Latin word *limen*, "threshold") is the ambiguity that emerges in the middle of fundamental transition. Liminality is the "in-between," where the space and participants no longer hold their past status but have not yet fully transformed to their post-transition self. —Anne-Laure Cunff, *Liminal Creativity*[7]

The day a CEO announces their resignation—whether of their own decision or not—is a milestone moment in an organization's history. It is a time of high vulnerability for the institution due to the challenges created by the need to appoint an effective interim director, manage effective internal and external communications, and appoint a search committee. Nonprofit leadership searches can take a full year, from the day a leader announces their departure to the day the new leader begins on the job. That year generates high levels of staff, board, and community anxiety about the future—and sometimes leads to unchecked bad behavior. It is important to acknowledge the ambiguity of this period but also to harness the opportunities for growth and new thinking.

The institutional transition period is one of liminality; people and organizations stand at the threshold of endings and then pass through an interim period before embarking on new beginnings. Folklorist Arnold van Gennep

(1873–1957) and anthropologist Victor Turner (1920–1983) both wrote about the cultural and ritual significance of these moments of transition. Van Gennep, who coined the term *liminality* in his 1909 book, *Rites of Passage*, highlighted the rituals that move individuals and groups through time, as they move from one state to another.[8] He describes pre-liminal rites, which mark a kind of symbolic death as old behaviors are left behind. Liminal rites are defined by the ceremonies that signify the movement from the old reality to the new, marking the crossing of a threshold or boundary. In the post-liminal rites, the individuals or collective begins anew, as a kind of rebirth.

The liminal stage of leadership change is also one of great opportunity for an institution as it can provide closure and the transition to an exciting future. While the period should be approached cautiously and with awareness of potential pitfalls, it should be looked upon as a time of advantage and rebirth. German philosopher Karl Jaspers wrote about an "Axial Age" in antiquity, describing it as a time of religious and philosophical change.[9] He referred to this period as "an interregnum between two ages of great empire, a pause for liberty, a deep breath bringing the most lucid consciousness."[10] Jaspers noted that as one period ended and another began, both the destruction and construction created opportunities for new thinking, traditions, and societal constructs.

> Life is in the transitions as much as in the terms connected. Often, indeed, it seems to be there more emphatically, as if our spurts and sallies forward were the real firing-line of the battle, were like the thin line of flame advancing across the dry autumnal field which the farmer proceeds to burn. In this line we live prospectively as well as retrospectively. It is "of" the past, inasmuch as it comes expressly as the past's continuation; it is "of" the future in so far as the future, when it comes, will have continued it. —William James, *A World of Pure Experience*[11]

Appropriate transitions are generally healthy for the leader and for the institution. In his quote above, James tells us that transitions are not just a means to an end; they can be the end themselves. Periods of transition are, in fact, a time of growth and opportunity for CEOs and for the institutions they lead. The time of transition, from the sallying forward to the firing line of battle, is a time for learning, risk-taking, and growth.

In *Life Is in the Transitions*, Bruce Feiler observes that a profound life transition lasts around five years, which is similar for an institution.[12] The change impact of the planning for departure, the departure, the arrival, and the transition to the leadership and vision of a new CEO also lasts around five years. We tend to think of all the events of a transition period as single activities or transactions, instead of understanding them as phases in a multiyear organizational transformation. And throughout this entire period, the people impacted undergo a plethora of emotions, experiencing many high and low points. The collective emotional toll on individuals in an institution is profound.

Feiler suggests that while life transitions are nonlinear, they have three phases: the long goodbye, the messy middle, and the new beginning. Noting that we tend to relish the phase that we are best at and bog down in the phase we find most difficult, Feiler suggests that in recognizing the phases of a transition, we can better anticipate the skills and attitudes that will help us move forward. He also notes that in our complex and volatile world, transitions are not occasional hiccups, but they are an integral part of life's continuity and an important part of what shapes our lives.[13] In her work on personal and professional transitions, Avivah Wittenberg-Cox writes that in life, we are always at some point in a state of "letting go of what was," embracing what's next (often unknown and ambiguous), and filled with fear, confusion, and uncertainty. She advises that we need pacing and planning; learning to leave gracefully; self-knowledge; and an understanding of the dynamic world around us.[14] The same is true for organizations as it is for individuals.

THE SEARCH

Search committees are formed and often include philanthropic trustees, patrons, and community representatives who are key stakeholders but may lack any experience in effective hiring. Inexperienced committee members often try to delegate their responsibility to search consultants, even though consultants are quick to point out that the analysis and selection of candidates can only be done by the search committee and board. A vacuum of leadership can emerge in these situations, causing search committees to fall back on looking for candidates who seem best able to replicate the past.

In 1987, the US Army War College adopted the acronym VUCA to describe the new world that was developing at the end of the twentieth century, following the fall of the Soviet Union and Cold War politics.[15] VUCA stands for:

- Volatile—unexpected and unstable challenges
- Uncertain—unpredicted challenges and outcomes
- Complex—interconnected and converged issues, situations, and interests
- Ambiguous—lacking clarity and precedents

The business world quickly adopted the VUCA concept as the impact of increased globalization, climate-change disasters, digital expansion, and political divisiveness changed their operating framework. Nonprofits are buoyed by the same vectors of change and also operate in a VUCA world. Whereas in the past, boards evaluated candidates almost exclusively for their subject matter expertise and charisma, today's criteria need to be expanded. Agility, which

I recently heard described as "the new intelligence," is now as important as field-related expertise.

Bill George, former CEO of Medtronic, wrote in *Forbes* that today's CEOs need to respond to a VUCA world as "VUCA leaders," which he describes as having:

- Vision—internalizing institutional values to create strategy.
- Understanding—using multiples sources and perspectives to understand the business and strategy.
- Courage—the ability to make bold and unexpected decisions in the face of changing circumstances.
- Adaptability—flexibility in a quickly changing world.[16]

I write this just after the global pandemic of COVID-19, the January 6th, 2021 attack on the Capitol, massive climate change–induced disasters, and the invasion of Ukraine—all widely unanticipated just five years ago. I couldn't have trained for the skills necessary for this time, and our board could not have hired me for experience managing unanticipated global emergencies. But what boards can and should hire for is a CEO with the vision, understanding, courage, and adaptability to navigate volatile, uncertain, complex, and unambiguous times.

Once the new executive is appointed, it is critical for the board members and the new director to begin with an intentional and strategic onboarding plan. Trustees are often unsure of how to help a new director, and they may confuse supportive guidance with aggressive oversight. Ultimately, the new CEO and the board members want to do the right thing, even if they are unsure what exactly that is. But, just as a pilot landing a plane, they cannot afford to leave the onboarding process to chance.

If *The Divine Comedy* teaches us anything, it is that we are sentient beings and that many of our life choices are shaped by human connections, emotions, and moral choices. We must therefore acknowledge that the period of a CEO transition is an emotional one for everyone, and the affective journey begins for the people involved the moment they anticipate change. Leadership transitions also enable both the CEO and the institution to break from the past and imagine a new future. It is a time for self-reflection and offers deeper understanding of an institution's potential.

NOTES

1. Dante Alighieri, *The Divine Comedy*, trans. by A. S. Kline. http://www.poetryintranslation.com/.

2. David L. Baker, quoted in Joel Stoller, "Managing Yourself: Single-Pilot Crew Resource Management," *Flight Training Magazine*, December 5, 2000, https://www.aopa.org/news-and-media/all-news/2000/december/flight-training-magazine/managing-yourself.

3. Dan Ciampa and Michael Watkins, *Right from the Start: Taking Charge in a New Leadership Role* (Boston: Harvard Business School Press, 1999), 15.

4. "Term Limits," BoardSource, accessed February 22, 2024, https://boardsource.org/resources/term-limits/.

5. Scott Keller, "Successfully Transitioning to New Leadership Roles," McKinsey & Company, May 23, 2018, https://www.mckinsey.com/capabilities/people-and-organizational-performance/our-insights/successfully-transitioning-to-new-leadership-roles#/.

6. Stephen R. Covey, *The 7 Habits of Highly Effective People* (New York: Free Press, 1989), 219–30.

7. Anne-Laure Cunff, "Liminal Creativity," accessed February 9, 2024, https://ness-labs.com/liminal-creativity.

8. Arnold van Gennep, *The Rites of Passage*, trans. by Monika B. Vizedom and Gabrielle L. Caffee (Chicago: University of Chicago Press, 2019).

9. Karl Jaspers, quoted in Karen Armstrong, *The Great Transformation: The Beginning of Our Religious Traditions* (New York: Knopf, 2006), 367.

10. Karl Jaspers, *The Origin and Goal of History*, trans. by Michael Bullock (London: Routledge & Keegan Paul, 1953), 51.

11. William James, "A World of Pure Experience," *Journal of Philosophy, Psychology and Scientific Methods*, Vol. 1, No. 20 (Sep. 29, 1904), 533–43, https://doi.org/10.2307/2011912.

12. Bruce Feiler, *Life Is in the Transitions: Mastering Change at Any Age* (New York: Penguin Press, 2020), 157.

13. Feiler, *Life Is in the Transitions*, 147–49.

14. Avivah Wittenberg-Cox, "Learn to Get Better at Transitions," *Harvard Business Review*, July 5, 2018, https://hbr.org/2018/07/learn-to-get-better-at-transitions.

15. Bill George, "VUCA 2.0: A Strategy for Steady Leadership in an Unsteady World," *Forbes*, February 17, 2017, https://www.forbes.com/sites/hbsworkingknowledge/2017/02/17/vuca-2-0-a-strategy-for-steady-leadership-in-an-unsteady-world/?sh=3c1951613d84.

16. George, "VUCA 2.0."

1

Succession Planning

For some leaders, talking about succession planning can feel like planning your own funeral. —Jeff Wahlstrom[1]

During an executive session of a board on which I serve, I asked my fellow trustees if we had a succession plan for the organization. I was told that the board president had a plan for his successor, but he hadn't shared it with anyone yet. I then asked about a plan for the CEO and was met with wide eyes and shocked silence. Someone mumbled that the CEO liked their job and planned to stay, so why even have the discussion? It was clear the CEO had never had a formal performance review. I asked about an emergency plan: What would we do if our CEO was suddenly unable to perform their duties? Who would step in? What was the communication plan? What were our vulnerabilities in this scenario? The discomfort in the room was palpable, and the conversation quickly changed to a discussion about a new roof for the building. Boards and CEOs are just not comfortable having the succession conversation.

We need to eliminate the funereal overtones and embrace the conversation about succession planning. At its core, it is simply a process to ensure the institution's continuity and successful future, come what may. As nonprofit institutions have increased in size and complexity, they have adopted many good practices from the corporate world, but succession planning is rarely one of those practices. Given that it is estimated that fewer than 40 percent of Americans have estate plans, perhaps it is not surprising that an even smaller percentage of nonprofits have succession plans.[2] Everyone prefers to ignore the inevitable, and boards and CEOs are loathe to answer the question. Just as we cannot avoid death or taxes, I can guarantee that every nonprofit's CEO will depart the organization at some point.

BoardSource estimates that only about a third of US nonprofits have a written succession plan in place, and the Society for Human Resource Management says only 22 percent of nonprofits have one.[3] Yet, as noted in the Stanford Social Innovation Review, succession planning is consistently recognized as the single greatest organizational concern of trustees and CEOs of nonprofits.[4] Whether it is a will, or a written succession plan, it is human nature to avoid expending resources on something with little pleasure or immediate return on investment, or to admit that we as individuals are expendable, no matter how long the intended lifespan of the nonprofit. Succession conversations will include big questions around performance, values, and an individual's future plans.

When I announced to the staff in Memphis that I was leaving the museum for another job, a senior staff member stood up and said, "We are very sorry to see you leave. We are happy for you, proud of you, and wish you well. But off you go. We are going to carry on along the path that you have set for us. We are on our way, and we will be wildly successful." At first, this message stung since I heard that I wasn't necessary for institutional success. But I quickly realized this was the very best response, emphasizing that the museum would continue to thrive without me at the helm. Ken Olsen, founder of Digital Equipment Corporation, once said, "There is only one measure of success and that is, five years after I'm gone, how is the company doing? I will accept no accolades until five years after I'm gone."[5] Leaving the organization poised to do even better in the years ahead under the next leader is the best indicator of a leader's success. The museum in Memphis would have been in an even better position for my departure if the board and I had developed a written succession plan.

PLANNING FOR THE INEVITABLE

Nonprofit institutions should always be planning for the departure of a CEO, whether sudden, planned, or not imminent. Anyone in need of a crystal ball to see the future should just consult the United States Census Bureau, which predicts that by 2030, all Baby Boomers will have passed retirement age, expanding the older generation so that one in every five people in the United States will be of retirement age.[6] The Boomer generation (people born between 1946 and 1964) is aging out of the workforce, and the New York Times has declared this "Gen X's moment" since the average age for most corporate CEOs is fifty-four.[7] As a Gen Xer, I am glad the New York Times has declared this my moment, but I also realize my generation is passing the mid-career mark and approaching career peaks. Within the next ten to fifteen years, we will be replaced by Millennials, the largest generation by population. While nothing is surprising in one generational cohort replacing another, we should be aware that it is always happening—meaning that organizations need to plan for transition with just as much predictability.

In addition to demographic changes, the United States is also experiencing behavioral changes, given "the Great Resignation" and the trend of career switching that we are experiencing in the wake of the COVID-19 pandemic. In 2021, an unprecedented forty-seven million Americans quit their jobs, which Joseph Fuller and William Kerr in the *Harvard Business Review* attribute to the "Five Rs: retirement, relocation, reconsideration (work-life balance), reshuffling, and reluctance (to return to in-person jobs)."[8] Pew Research found that in 2022, 53 percent of people who left their jobs did so to make a change of occupation, and one in five workers anticipate making a career change in the near future.[9] Decisions have been encouraged by the stock market, increased property values, and the aging of Baby Boomers. People prioritizing their work-life balance, job satisfaction, and sense of purpose will be a lasting effect of the global pandemic on the workforce, even if other factors recede. Climate change and artificial intelligence will likely have further effects on employment longevity that we cannot yet anticipate.

I served on the board of an organization with a long-serving director who never gave the organization any indication of their retirement plans. During every executive session of the board and every meeting of the governance and nominating committee meetings, we would second-guess their plans, worrying about the future of the organization if they stayed much longer—or if they up and left suddenly. Because there was no succession plan and the CEO didn't share their plans, the board felt forced to resolve the situation and, unfortunately, it turned ugly.

The CEO later told the board that we should have just asked them for their plans, and they would have shared them. Given the sensitivity of discussions of age and the word *retirement*, it is much healthier for a board to have a stated succession planning requirement from CEOs, articulated from the CEO's appointment, to reduce the risk of misunderstandings, hurt feelings, and lawyers.

It is hard for CEOs not to take a succession discussion personally and to assume that such a request coming from a board is an indication of board displeasure. Nobody wants to be seen as a "lame duck" or feel that their authority is being compromised. If a CEO introduces the topic, trustees become concerned that their leader is planning a departure (even if they say they aren't). And as soon as the topic is introduced, trustees and staff become concerned that by calling the question, they are ushering in a radical change of direction. It is not uncommon in nonprofit organizations that the CEO's identity and the institution merge, adding greater sensitivity to an already-sensitive process.

The best way to ensure that a succession plan is understood to be what it is—a tool to ensure that an organization performs at its best during its most vulnerable and uncertain time—is to ensure that the responsibility is included in the charter of a board committee. The function is best suited to the work of a governance and compensation committee since succession planning is most closely aligned to the performance and compensation review of the CEO and senior staff. Due to the confidential and personal nature of the work, it can also be a part of the work of an executive committee. The topic of succession planning should be introduced to a new CEO in their first year, so that it is understood that the institution recognizes that this is best business practice, and nothing personal.

A board's most important responsibility is to hire, evaluate, and sometimes fire the CEO. To help the board carry out this function, the CEO must ensure a robust annual evaluation process. I am still surprised by the number of non-profits that do not have a formal CEO review process, which is not good for the CEO or the organization. A good review process should include the CEO's formal written self-evaluation about progress on goals during the year ending and a list of goals for the year ahead. Wherever possible, it should be specific and include goals that can be measured. I always include a narrative in my annual self-evaluation that "tells the story" of the year's work and includes leadership challenges and successes that are harder to quantify. The best reviews offer the entire board and the leadership team the opportunity to weigh in, but the final performance analysis should be done by board leadership.

Ideally, succession planning should be an iterative process. Each new CEO is a milestone in the long history of an organization, and the board should always be anticipating the next milestone. This sort of long view is a reminder that we are all temporary stewards, whose job is to leave an organization better than we found it and positioned for future success. It is the board's job to play the long game, thinking one or two CEOs ahead and assessing internal and external talent. Requiring an annually updated succession plan from the CEO and responsible committee helps to depersonalize the succession process and ensure that the plan is current.

IT'S THE TALENT, STUPID

To riff on James Carville's 1992 often-quoted comment, "It's the economy, stupid," it really is the talent.[10] A good succession plan is a talent assessment and development strategy, ensuring that the institution is always addressing talent gaps and nurturing leadership growth in its staff. Referring to a "leadership deficit," the Stanford Social Innovation Review notes that only 30 percent of C-suite roles in the nonprofit sector were filled by internal candidates, which is about half of that in the corporate world.[11] A recent report from search consultants Russell Reynolds reports that 77 percent of corporate CEOs who started a new role in 2023 were internal appointments, which they credit to strong succession planning.[12] We are simply not investing enough resources in the growth of our internal talent pool, and it holds nonprofits back in multiple ways.

Years ago, I learned from a diversity and inclusion officer to adopt a strategy she called "always be recruiting" (ABR). The point is that we all encounter talented individuals frequently and in a variety of contexts, and we should always have our antennas up for these interactions. I am a keen observer of talent at all levels, always scouting for leaders and managers with emotional intelligence, curiosity, and talent. Recognizing and recruiting talent has been the secret to any success I have had as a director. I never lose sight of the talented people I have encountered along the path of my thirty-year career. I stay in touch with the impressive people whom I work with, both internal and external to my organization, and I am always thinking about opportunities to work together, even if it is in a different context. I can match people to roles in an organization that they wouldn't have considered for themselves until receiving my phone call because I watch for the "soft skills" and leadership talent.

A talent strategy is critical in expanding an institution's capabilities for current business challenges as well as preparing the organization for the future. It is the responsibility of the CEO to develop the next two levels of talent so that the organization is always nurturing future leaders. When I leave my current role, it will be the board's decision whether to hire an internal or external candidate, but it is my responsibility to ensure there are multiple internal options for them to consider.

Leadership development cannot be left to chance or delegated to human resources staff; the director must ensure that a dynamic and strategic talent program is in place. The plan should include effective annual performance evaluations; development goals; regular two-way feedback loops; formal and informal training programs; coaching; and annual projects that stretch an employee. An effective leader nurtures lifelong learners and fosters an abundance mindset. Trustees should ensure that leadership is actively updating and engaging the board on the topic of talent development.

This strategy extends to senior and middle managers, who should be preparing for leadership needs even further in the future. The formality of writing and approving a plan holds everyone accountable for following a professional talent strategy that supports the success of the institution, for the short and long term. Nonprofit leaders sometimes assume that they cannot afford training for their staff, but there are countless ways to support learning and growth. Trustees, stakeholders, and community leaders are often willing to share their expertise in formal and informal gatherings, offering seminars to develop staff. An active learning program can include the circulation of books and articles and participation in inexpensive online seminars can be encouraged. Senior leaders who support learning and growth across the institution help to develop an organization-wide culture of curiosity and a growth mindset. People who feel that learning and growth are part of their employee experience are also much more likely to stay.

COMPONENTS OF A SUCCESSION PLAN

Succession plans come in many forms and will be organic to the institution they are serving. Writing a plan to cover sudden emergencies is the most important part of a succession plan and is where every CEO should start. Anyone looking for a template can find countless examples in books, articles, and online sources.

The Chicken Truck Plan

Since living in the South, I have always referred to the emergency plan should I, or a member of the leadership team, die or become suddenly incapacitated, as a "chicken truck plan." The image of a truck stuffed with chickens, coupled with its unlikeliness (especially in Washington, D.C.) adds some humor to an otherwise-macabre consideration. A chicken truck plan is an emergency backup plan, and every organization needs one. If your organization does not have one, stop reading this book and write one.

The emergency chicken truck plan will cover both short- and long-term unexpected absences of the CEO and key leadership team members and can be a brief document. But it should be a document and not simply something that lives in the CEO's head—chicken trucks cause head injuries, too. Essential ingredients of this plan include the following:

Name(s) of proposed interim CEO and the reasoning behind the decision

The CEO and board should agree on the proposed interim CEO and the rationale for why this individual's strengths would serve the institution during the traumatic time of an unplanned absence of the CEO. This person may or may not be a candidate to eventually replace the CEO, but that is not the decision at hand. It is best practice to identify a second person who could take over if the first-choice person is unable to serve.

Key responsibilities of the interim CEO

It is important to recognize that an interim CEO is unlikely to have all the skills, experience, contacts, and characteristics of the current CEO. The plan, therefore, should articulate the key duties of the interim leader, taking into consideration whether the CEO will be returning anytime soon. In many cases, the institution may want to identify co-interim CEOs. If a single interim CEO cannot be identified, leadership should understand that the lack of an identified heir-apparent should shape the institution's talent strategy going forward. What training must be done to ensure that within a defined period, one or more potential CEOs are being developed?

The person who will absorb some of the interim CEO's current responsibilities

Given that it is unlikely that the interim CEO can fully continue their normal duties in their temporary new role, the document should include a plan for sharing or absorbing those duties elsewhere. Once again, any weaknesses in a potential successor to the interim CEO should be identified in an institutional talent strategy for growth.

Will the role of other leadership team members change with a temporary CEO in place?

Assuming that the chicken truck may completely incapacitate the sitting CEO, the plan should include an analysis of the rest of the senior talent. Nobody knows the strengths, weaknesses, and potential of the senior team as well as the incapacitated CEO, so the plan for the deployment of current talent should be recorded in advance.

Robust communication plan

The document should outline a plan for internal communication, listed by urgency: key trustees and staff; the full board; the full staff; and volunteers. External stakeholder categories should be considered, such as donors, elected officials, vendors, and community groups, along with the person or role responsible for the communication to these groups. Finally, consideration should be given to a wider public announcement, including media and the press. It is critical to develop the communication plan before an emergency because, in the thick of a crisis, key stakeholders can be overlooked.

DEPARTURE-DEFINED SUCCESSION PLANNING

Having successfully dodged the chicken truck, the best form of succession planning occurs when a CEO announces they will leave or retire in six to eighteen months (which rarely occurs). With the benefit of time, the CEO and board can work together on a transition plan. In the best-case scenario, this means revisiting and updating the current succession plan. The most important work of the CEO during this time is to wrap up legacy projects and ensure the conditions are in place for their successor's success. A departing CEO will want to work with the board to identify and resolve some short-term issues, such as:

- Identify and settle outstanding human resource problems.
- Identify and resolve governance problems at the board level.
- Assess the current strategic plan and define short- and long-term organizational priorities.
- Identify greatest opportunities and threats before the organization for the next three to five years.
- Prepare the organization for an executive search.

BUILDING THE PLAN

Succession plans can take many forms, but they should include the following topics:

- Plan for an unanticipated emergency that removes the CEO from office, temporarily or permanently (the "chicken truck plan")
- Comprehensive transition communications plan (internal and external)
- Assessment of current leadership needs/traits
- CEO position description
- CEO evaluation philosophy and process
- List of potential search consultants
- Updated organization chart
- Description of board responsibilities
- Staff talent analysis, including potential internal candidates
- Mentorship and leadership development program
- Onboarding plan for a new CEO
- List of the ten things the current CEO wishes they had known before taking the job
- List of the ten nagging challenges the current CEO should resolve before departure
- Succession plan for additional key leadership positions

NOTES

1. Jeff Wahlstrom, "Succession Planning Should Not Be Confused with Funeral Planning," Starboard Leadership Consulting, LLC, accessed February 23, 2024, https://www.starboardleadership.com/leadership-transitions/succession-planning-should-not-be-confused-with-funeral-planning/.
2. Lorie Konish, "67 percent of Americans have no estate plan, survey finds. Here's how to get started on one," CNBC, published April 11, 2022, https://www.cnbc.com/2022/04/11/67percent-of-americans-have-no-estate-plan-heres-how-to-get-started-on-one.html.
3. Robin Hindsman Stacia, PsyD., and Lita Pardi, "Address the Need for Nonprofit Succession Planning," BoardSource Blog, July 27, 2016, https://blog.boardsource.org/blog/address-the-need-for-nonprofit-succession-planning; Emily Douglas-McNab, "Succession Planning 101," *Education Week*, November 6, 2012, https://www.edweek.org/leadership/opinion-succession-planning-101/2012/11.
4. Libbie Landles-Cobb, Kirk Kramer, and Kate Smith Milway, "The Nonprofit Leadership Development Deficit," *Stanford Social Innovation Review*, October 22, 2015, https://ssir.org/articles/entry/the_nonprofit_leadership_development_deficit.
5. Glen Rifkin, "Making a Difference; Mr. Olsen Hangs On . . . ," *New York Times*, November 10, 1991, https://www.nytimes.com/1991/11/10/business/making-a-difference-mr-olsen-hangs-on.html.

6. "Older People Projected to Outnumber Children for First Time in U.S. History," United States Census Bureau, last modified October 8, 2019, https://www.census.gov/newsroom/press-releases/2018/cb18-41-population-projections.html.
7. Emma Goldberg, "Gen X Is in Charge. Don't Make a Big Deal About It," *New York Times*, July 7, 2023, https://www.nytimes.com/2023/07/07/business/gen-x-in-charge-companies-chief-executives.html.
8. Joseph Fuller and William Kerr, "The Great Resignation Didn't Start with the Pandemic," *Harvard Business Review*, March 23, 2022, https://hbr.org/2022/03/the-great-resignation-didnt-start-with-the-pandemic.
9. Rakesh Kochhar, Kim Parker, and Ruth Igielnik, "Majority of U.S. Workers Changing Jobs Are Seeing Real Wage Gains," Pew Research Center, July 28, 2022, https://www.pewresearch.org/social-trends/2022/07/28/majority-of-u-s-workers-changing-jobs-are-seeing-real-wage-gains/.
10. James Carville, Political Dictionary, https://politicaldictionary.com/words/its-the-economy-stupid/.
11. Landles-Cobb, Kramer, and Smith Milway, "The Nonprofit Leadership Development Deficit."
12. Russell Reynolds, "Global CEO Turnover Index," accessed February 23, 2024, https://www.russellreynolds.com/en/insights/reports-surveys/global-ceo-turnover-index.

2

The Departure

All leaders have a shelf life. We don't want to hear it, but it's true. While there is no hard and fast rule for the optimal nonprofit CEO tenure, I believe it to be roughly a decade, give or take a few years on either side. There are plenty of successful cases of both shorter and longer tenures, so there are exceptions to this timeline. Nobody wants to outstay their welcome, and we should be attuned to the internal and external signs of the opportune time for change. Everyone wants the departure to occur when the party is still fun.

Great institutions have been built by the influx of new talent and vision. We are all just bricks in the walls of our organizations, adding strength, structure, and texture to each course, all the while making the institution stronger and better. Danger occurs when leaders think they are the architect, contractor, and the wall. Leaders who stay too long sometimes become the institution, which isn't healthy for them or the organization. I know many leaders who, facing retirement, decide to stay on longer because they are not sure who they would be without their career identity. While this concern is common to many leaders, it is not a reason to stay, and it too often forces a board to make the decision for the CEO.

Leaders can become too comfortable in their roles and stop pushing themselves and the organization. Boredom sometimes leads to distractions— "let's open a satellite institution!"—and a slowing of innovation. An enervated leader's boredom permeates the staff, frustrates the board, shortchanges the community, and shrinks institutional ambitions. Burnout is another symptom that the passion for the work has diminished, and it is often discernible to stakeholders.

Boards have a paradoxical relationship with long-serving directors. They sometimes work to hang on too long to leaders because they are afraid of what change might bring. Their commitment is sometimes less about belief that an individual is the right leader for the time and more about the fear that a search might produce someone worse (which would reflect poorly on them). Given the amount of healthy board turnover and lack of experience with a search, boards will often put up with a lot to avoid an unfamiliar process with an uncertain result. Over time, trustees naturally become friends with directors, blurring their judgment and compromising their governance roles. It is even more difficult to decide when to make a change when an institution has a long-serving founder, as both the board and the founder can feel entitled to an extended tenure.

Boards can also become frustrated by the confidence and security of long-serving directors. Trustees like to feel that they are needed, and as directors ascend to the comfort level of a long tenure, they are more secure in their actions and community network and less reliant on trustees. The early years of a director's tenure are generally a bit rocky as the new leader takes the place out for a spin, and staff, stakeholders, and the media watch the director with trained binoculars. Trustee engagement is usually higher during this period because CEOs are more reliant on trustees for advice and community connections. Longer-serving directors tend to experience fewer crises, and the institution settles into its new comfortable normalcy. Trustees can feel sidelined when a long-serving and confident director works more independently, even if the action is not deliberate. Emergencies draw boards together, making trustees feel useful and engaged in problem-solving.

When things run smoothly for some time, trustees sometimes feel extraneous and resentful. I have heard trustees of multiple organizations say, "I don't feel my talents are being used right now." Although this phrase usually comes from people with an unrealistic sense of the usefulness of their talents, it is true that they feel less engaged when operations run with efficiency and effectiveness. We don't like to admit it, but the tension between a "hungry" and vulnerable director who has the drive to prove themselves and trustees who are invested in the developing success of a relatively new leader is healthy, and this is where institutions can enjoy exciting success. CEOs shouldn't let tenure and comfort lead to complacency.

When a leader is building their track record, they can be more demanding of institutional talent. On several occasions, as I have prepared to depart an institution, I have realized that I was leaving one or two challenging human-resource issues for my successor, even though I had developed my own system to manage these individuals. After a while, we overlook problematic qualities in certain employees as we have accepted them, often working around the problems or compensating for them ourselves. On more than one occasion, as my departure neared, I realized that what was an occasional frustration for me could be a liability for the next person.

HOW DO YOU KNOW WHEN IT IS TIME TO LEAVE?

According to the Bureau of Labor Statistics (BLS), in 2022 the average tenure of workers in management and professional roles was five years.[1] In fact, every five years or so, it is healthy to take a formal career temperature check. Move off the dance floor and head up to the balcony to survey the dance. As you consider tenure and career longevity, you want to leave when you are still having fun at the dance. If you have reached the stage where you are bored, are regularly irritated by routine challenges, are abnormally frustrated by the board, or have stopped innovating, it is time to move on. If you think the institution cannot thrive without you, it is also time to go.

The worst situation occurs when you realize this state too late, and the board is forced to make the change for you. Don't let that person be you; keep a close read on the board and listen to your advisors. Watch out for the trustee parking lot huddles. Use succession planning to have honest conversations with board leadership about your career plans.

When I was twenty-eight and working as a curator at a small museum in Fresno, a trustee called me one day at work and asked me to come see him the next day. The museum was struggling over a conflicted purpose and poor finances, and the director clearly wasn't a good fit. After a few minutes in his office, the trustee said, "I am going to get the director fired, and I need someone else to do the job. Can *you* do it?" I confirmed that I could, and he told me to bring him a business plan for the museum. I went home and called my father to ask how to write a business plan.

I was appointed the director of the museum about four months later. My father was never a person to let a life lesson go to waste, and he urged me to learn from this experience about how boards work, even though I was the beneficiary in this situation. He told me to always remain alert and attuned to their behavior, in the boardroom and outside of it. Always read the room. You may feel confident that you know what they are thinking as individuals, but something happens when they assemble as a group in a room, behind closed doors. I learned from my Fresno experience that in certain conditions, a single trustee can change an institution.

In deciding when it is time to leave, be sure that you are not running away from something, but running to something. Some questions you might consider during your five-year career check-in include:

* Am I Still Taking Risks and Urging the Institution into a New Future?
  I describe myself as an informed risk-taker. The most important part of the risk-taking process is consideration of the downside. What is the cost of complete failure, and can you afford it? If you can't afford it, don't take that risk. But if you can survive complete failure and chances of success are good, you should be taking the risk. In our volatile, uncertain, complex, and

ambiguous world, the status quo is often the riskiest place to be. We tend to take more risks earlier in our tenures and fewer as we become safer and more settled. Are you still kicking the tires on the status quo?

- What Does the Next Level Look Like for This Organization? Can I Even See It Anymore?

  While "going to the next level" is a vague description, we know it when we see it. It can include many elements, but it should include the necessary steps to increase a nonprofit's impact on its audiences and clients. For-profit businesses exist to return financial value to shareholders, while nonprofits serve a public benefit mission. We should always be challenging ourselves to envision the institution's next great step to exponentially expand public benefit. Building new buildings should not be the default to increase public benefit.

- Am I Still Seeking Feedback and Listening to Criticism for Lessons?

  All leaders suffer from a feedback deficit. Too few of us solicit feedback widely, and few people want to give it to us. In their excellent book, *Thanks for the Feedback*, Douglas Stone and Sheila Heen define *feedback* as "any information you get about yourself. In the broadest sense it's how we learn about ourselves from our experiences and from other people—how we learn from life."[2] Leaders must work harder to get meaningful feedback from staff and stakeholders; they just don't believe we want to hear it; they feel certain it will negatively impact their job if they are honest; and they don't think we will change anyway.

  Stone and Heen have identified three triggers that cause strong reactions to feedback: truth triggers; relationship triggers; and identity triggers. The authors note that reactions to these triggers are perfectly normal, but they can keep us from really listening and learning.[3] We must cultivate a "growth identity," in which we see ourselves as ever evolving and growing.[4] Complacency is the enemy of excellence. We must always strive to be better—and feedback from peers, subordinates, and coaches is a critical way to get better. Darwin Smith, the twenty-year CEO of Kimberly-Clark said, "I never stopped trying to be qualified for the job."[5]

- Is the Leadership Team Performing at a High Level? Am I Challenging and Inspiring Them?

  It generally takes several years for a CEO to assemble their own high-functioning leadership team, and there are often some hiccups along the way. It then takes time for the leadership to gel as a high-functioning team. Complacency settles into teams as well as individuals, so the CEO must always be pushing the team to innovate and challenge each other.

- Are Our Strategies Driven by the Public's Greater Needs?

  Legendary director of the Wadsworth Athenaeum A. Everett (Chick) Austin allegedly used to say, "The role of an art museum is to amuse the director." Whenever I repeat the quip, I notice that some people smile mildly and quite a few people roll their eyes. Because of the fundraising demands for most nonprofit leadership, the field tends to cultivate charismatic leaders and impresarios. This is fair enough, but we need to keep the focus not on our own egos and interests or the needs of the institution, but on the needs of the audiences we serve. I have seen far too many unsuccessful museum expansions that were initiated out of a combination of boredom and ego.

- Am I Too Reliant on Too Few People?

    It is critical to have a small team of trusted advisors who will give you the feedback and information that you need to hear. It is also important, however, to keep widening your net of connections so that you see issues from multiple perspectives. I am a big fan of Bryan Stevenson, lawyer and founder of the Equal Justice Initiative in Montgomery, Alabama. In his outline of the four steps to make the United States a more just and equitable world, Stevenson urges us all to "get proximate" to people with a lived experience unlike our own.[6] We all benefit and grow from getting to know people whose lived experience is different from our own. If we isolate ourselves in our own small network, it is much harder to grow and stimulate new thinking. Watch out for echo chambers. Leaders have a hard time getting honest feedback from employees; they have to work hard at it and remain vigilant.

- How Often Do I Wake Up and Dread Going to Work?

    While working in London years ago, a colleague who frequently found reasons not to come to work called to say he couldn't come into work because "the duvet was too heavy to move." We all have days when that duvet feels a bit weighty, but if those days stack up, it is time to think of a move. Ask yourself often not only if you love the job, but whether you also feel energized by the work.

- Are There Challenges Out There That We Have Not Yet Tackled? Am I the One to Take Them On?

    Being faced with a looming and unavoidable facility crisis, major capital campaign, or significant staff or board reorganization is often the trigger point for nonprofit leaders to move on. As we look out at a major project that will require most of the leader's time and energy over many years, it is natural to ask if that work should be left to the next CEO. The critical part is to always be thinking about strategy and opportunities that will present themselves in the future. We do the institution a disservice if we push off necessary major projects too long because we don't want to do them, but we also aren't ready to leave.

- Has My Relationship with the Board Soured?

    Some nonprofits have huge boards, and it can be hard to keep such a large and divergent group happy, engaged, and supportive. So much of a nonprofit CEO's job is managing the board, and it can be exhausting and not always productive. There are occasions when a series of cascading events erode the trust and collegiality between the CEO and some trustees. CEOs need to read the boardroom carefully and make the decision to leave before it is made for them. If you are in this situation, be sure to learn from it so that you don't find yourself in the same situation at your next job. We can often learn more from bad bosses than good bosses.

- How Much of My Daily Work Gives Me Energy? How Much of It Drains My Energy? Can I Increase Energy and Decrease the Drain?

    Every now and then I notice that work doesn't feel joyful for days or weeks in succession. In those moments, I conduct a written personal energy audit. I make a list of what I do that noticeably energizes me. I also list what I do that is neutral, with little or no impact on my energy level. And then I ponder what activities diminish my energy. I review the list and consider how I can eliminate or delegate tasks that drain my energy, minimize the neutral ones, and expand the ones that elevate my energy. This is important awareness for a CEO because our personal value proposition as leaders lies in the energy that drives our work. That's where we move beyond a caretaker leader to a leader who takes the organization to the next level. If you complete the energy audit and cannot find your way to a position of high energy, it may be time to think about a change.

- Will a New Opportunity Enlarge Me?

    In his *Eight Secrets to a (Fairly) Fulfilled Life* column for the *Guardian*, Oliver Burkeman suggests we look at opportunities through the lens of "will this enlarge me?" instead of "will this make me happy?"[7] Ultimately, there is no single or "right" career path out there for any of us. Serendipity is often the real road we drive along, but we often come to a crossroads. According to Burkeman, "We're terrible at predicting what will make us happy: the question swiftly gets bogged down in our narrow preferences for security and control. But the enlargement question elicits a deeper, intuitive response. You tend to just *know* whether, say, leaving or remaining in a relationship or a job, though it might bring short-term comfort, would mean cheating yourself of growth."[8]

- Do I See the Organization through the Eyes of Abundance or Scarcity?

    Related to the earlier question of energy, successful leaders bring a view of abundance to their work. Leadership guru Stephen Covey coined the term *abundance mentality* in his popular book *The Seven Habits of Highly Successful People*.[9] Covey argues that great leaders see that there are plenty of resources and reward for others, instead of hoarding for themselves. An abundance mentality is one of generosity, one that looks at a half-full glass as one filled with resources and opportunity for all. Someone who sees scarcity sees limitations. They avoid sharing credit or feeling happiness for the success of others. A leader with an abundant mindset is one who authentically projects joy, satisfaction, and optimism for others and for the work of the institution. Matthew Teitelbaum, director of the Boston Museum of Fine Art, likes to say, "The more we give away, the richer we are."

- Am I Still Learning? Am I Still Teaching?

    The best job experiences are the ones that enable us to grow personally and professionally. That growth should be a combination of professional expertise, skills, experiences, and expanded horizons that leads to greater self-awareness, expanded empathy, and expansive curiosity. To be able to grow as part of our employment is a privilege and a gift. We owe it to our organizations to pass the gift along, nurturing our colleagues' curiosity and inspiring them to keep learning and growing.

- Am I Yearning for a Sabbatical?

    Ninety percent of the nonprofit leaders I know who have taken sabbaticals resigned shortly after their return. If you are yearning for an extended break to reignite your passion for the work, interrogate the impulse. It just might be time for a change.

No matter how talented a leader you are, your honest answers to the questions above could help direct your decision about when it is time to leave. We shortchange ourselves and our institutions when we are complacent and not at our absolute game-day best. People in leadership roles who are institutional caretakers are not actually leading. If you are not working hard to advance the mission and expand the impact of our work, you are in the wrong role.

WHEN THE RECRUITER RINGS

After I had been at the museum in Memphis for many years, my answers to some of the questions above indicated to me that it was time to think about my next move. To this day, I can still hear my practical father saying, "The best time to think about a new job is when you still have one." I can remember the excitement of seeing the red blinking message light on my desk phone at work and then hearing the voice of search consultant Malcolm MacKay saying, "Kaywin, it's Malcolm. Love a callback." Always discreet, Malcolm would never say which opportunity he was calling about, making the prospect of discovery more exciting. Malcolm, dubbed a "kingmaker" by the New York Times in 2004 for filling so many important museum director jobs (it was still very much a "king's" world), believed in me and supported my candidacy in several interesting searches.[10] In fact, I owe a lot of my career to him because his advocacy put me in searches for which I probably wouldn't otherwise have been considered. There's a lesson here: develop relationships with major search consultants in your field (and always be good to their administrative assistants).

A search consultant taught me early in my career that if you have absolutely no interest in a role, you should not take an interview. But if you even have a marginal interest, you should at least explore it, and if something is intriguing about it, go for an interview. At the very least, you will gain additional interview experience, and even if you decline the opportunity, you will have left behind an influential group of people impressed by you. I still cross paths with trustees I met on searches and am glad to have maintained good relationships. In graduate school, my PhD supervisor told me, "Be careful how you treat people on your way up; you will see them again on your way back down." If you work in a nonprofit, your field is likely quite insular, and you will see some of the same people coming and going. It is always good to be on the good radar of influential people.

Understandably, boards do not like to hear that their CEO is interviewing. No matter how much a search consultant assures you of confidentiality, it is always a risk. Before going into a second-round discussion with a board, it can be good to have a quiet word with the board chairperson if you have a good relationship. I do so because mutual trust is an important part of my relationship with a chair. But this strategy depends on the rapport with the chair; it can definitely backfire.

ANNOUNCING THE DEPARTURE

Once a contract or agreement has been negotiated with your future employer, it is time to set the departure in motion. After consulting your succession plan, you should discuss implications for the staff, funding, and pending big projects with the board chair and key trustees. You will want to identify any large or unusual challenges that your departure might create. Trustees will immediately look for solutions and guidance on the way forward: search consultants, interim leadership, and resources needed for a search.

This is a complex process as it involves planning across two institutions, and it can feel like a scene from a movie where the actor has a left foot firmly on one train car and the right foot on another. As they stare at the moving ground below, the train is about to mount a bend. At this moment, you feel precariously perched between two moving worlds and pulled in different directions. You will naturally feel conflicted loyalties, although your gut is to prioritize the current employer. A search consultant once gave me some tough love and advised me to prioritize my new institution as it now represented my future, and nobody should start with a misstep. At the end of the day, you will have to make choices because not everyone can hear the news at the exact same time. There will need to be well-timed cascading announcements across both institutions.

There will be two different but related press releases for the two institutions. Although one release will be retrospective and the other prospective, both releases will summarize the CEO's strengths and achievements and include quotes about the CEO from trustees in each institution. At the CEO's current institution, the quote from the board chair will emphasize stability, a search, and an exciting future. The quote from the incoming CEO should contain praise for the outgoing CEO they are replacing, and for the staff, stakeholders, and community they look forward to working with. The golden rule of all departures and arrivals is to be radically gracious. Generous heaps of praise must go to everyone else who made the success of your tenure possible and to the people with whom you will soon be working.

As you plan your departure announcement at one institution and arrival at another, you will likely work in confidence with the public relations officer at both institutions to develop a schedule. This schedule will include an outline of key communications actions, whom the intended audience is for each communication, who is responsible for it, and all related due dates. Plans should include stakeholder phone and email lists, newsletter lists, and media lists. The departing CEO, the board chair, and the head of communications should develop a one-page list of key talking points about the CEO's tenure and the transition and search processes.

Generally, the announcement of your departure will begin with trustees, followed by any critical donors. The staff announcement generally lands just before the press release embargo is lifted. Because you cannot tell everyone all at once, just know that some people will be hurt that they heard the news from someone else, so be thoughtful as you plan out the progression of your phone calls. Don't leave it to chance—plan every call and contact in advance. Since the director will not be able to contact all appropriate donors and stakeholders, there should also be a plan for trustees, senior staff, and development professionals to make calls.

I have always met with the staff in person to share the news of my departure. It's a difficult meeting, filled with emotions. Your job is to inform with the facts and then to emphasize security and stability for the institution in the weeks and months ahead. The staff quickly moves from surprise to concern about what the news means for them. Their worries extend to both the interim period before a new director (if no successor is announced immediately) and to the potential life change before them with a new CEO. Poorly managed departures can lead to a decrease in staff productivity, loss of focus, and the departure of talent. If the current CEO is departing suddenly and under duress, there will be even greater strain on the institution, and communication becomes even more important. In these unfortunate cases, the board must have a very strong presence in all internal and external communications about the departure and should expect to spend more time with the staff than during a voluntary planned departure.

Within the next day or two, you will be heading off to meet the staff at your next opportunity, which can be brutal on the heels of the emotional announcement at your current institution (and you still have a foot on each car of the moving trains). It is at this point, my husband reminds me, that most airline accidents happen—at takeoff and landing. You need to plan your exit carefully and keep your focus on the people impacted. Likewise, you need to recognize that when you first arrive at your new institution as their future leader, everyone is watching you carefully, examining your body language, attire, interactions, and absolutely everything you say. It can be exhausting.

Departing CEOs should expect waves of difficult emotions. In addition to the sadness of saying goodbye and the anxieties we feel around a new beginning, there is the discomfort of being torn between two institutions. Lame duck never feels good for anyone, but nonprofit boards often ask for several months' notice before the CEO leaves. During that period, you feel your current institution slipping away from you as staff and trustees sometimes leave you out of future-focused discussions. You will also be subjected to occasional hints that you are disloyal for "abandoning" the institution. But you do not yet feel a part of your new institution, so you feel like you are between two worlds, not fully belonging to either. The worst of it happens shortly after you announce your departure, when people aren't sure what this new state means. Things soon settle in again as the transition state becomes your norm.

NOTES

1. Bureau of Labor Statistics, "Employee Tenure in 2022," accessed August 17, 2023, https://www.bls.gov/news.release/pdf/tenure.pdf.
2. Douglas Stone and Sheila Heen, *Thanks for the Feedback* (New York: Penguin, 2014), 4.
3. Stone and Heen, *Thanks for the Feedback*, 16.
4. Stone and Heen, *Thanks for the Feedback*, 24.
5. Carol S. Dweck, *Mindset: The New Psychology of Success* (New York: Ballantine Book, 2016), 20.
6. Bryan Stevenson, "The Power of Proximity," YouTube video, 34:15, June 26, 2018, https://www.youtube.com/watch?v=1RyAwZIHo4Y.
7. Oliver Burkeman, "The Eight Secrets to a (Fairly) Fulfilled Life," *Guardian*, September 4, 2020, https://www.theguardian.com/lifeandstyle/2020/sep/04/oliver-burke-mans-last-column-the-eight-secrets-to-a-fairly-fulfilled-life.
8. Burkeman, "The Eight Secrets."
9. Covey, *The 7 Habits*, 219–30.
10. Tom Mullaney, "ART: The Museum World's Kingmaker Crowns Again," *New York Times*, April 25, 2004, https://www.nytimes.com/2004/04/25/arts/art-the-museum-world-s-kingmaker-crowns-again.html.

3

The Search

Writing about the onboarding of Harvard's next president after the six-month failed tenure of Claudine Gay, George Bradt urges Harvard's board to be deliberate in their search and onboarding. He argues for the importance of aligning the board around the key priorities, threats, and opportunities the new president will face. The board needs to be brutally honest about the challenges the new president will face. They need to help the next leader by resolving some of the burning problems at hand. Finally, they need to help the president identify the most important stakeholders who will need the leader's attention and help the president to accelerate the work with prioritization and wise counsel.[1]

Bradt's argument is that the board's role in searching for a new leader is not simply to conduct a search and then host a welcome cocktail party. All boards need to do significant internal work and institutional soul-searching even before they start the search. It is a time to learn more about the institution they steward and identify key priorities and risks the individual will face. Once the new leader is on board, their job is to ensure their success, which requires wise counsel, generous sharing of contacts, vocal and visible advocacy, and thoughtful support for new directions.

INTERIM LEADERSHIP

The first challenge to confront a board is the selection of interim leadership. If the succession plan is up-to-date, this will be an easy and already-well-considered part of the process. If there is no succession plan in place, the conversation generally starts with the board chair and the departing CEO and then proceeds to the executive committee.

The most important part of this process is to recognize that anxieties are extremely high across the staff and board. Fears, including among trustees, are commonly rooted in concerns about a loss of power and influence. Staff members fear that someone with poor leadership capabilities or someone internal who is threatening to their position will be selected. Boards struggle with the option of selecting a senior leader with expertise in the nonprofit's mission (e.g., a curator in a museum) or an operations and finance specialist. My advice is always to go with the operations person. In the interim period, it is more likely that the institution will have operational challenges than mission service challenges. Boards need to remember that they are not hiring a CEO, but a temporary leader to carry through the operational moment. Many times, there is not just one right person, and while a co-interim leadership position is rarely the best solution, it can work. I have seen boards select co-interim directors because they don't want to upset a trustee or major donor who has a favorite staff member, but it is one who isn't qualified. This is not a good reason to have co-interim leaders. It is also important that the two leaders have a good working relationship, as shared authority is challenging in the best of times. Trustees shouldn't assume this is the case.

The worst solution boards make is to select a trustee to serve as the interim director. Boards love the solution of a trustee serving as interim, assuming that one of them could do a better job than any nonprofit leader and that the organization will be safer during this interim period because the board is in charge. Because the corporate world often views nonprofit leadership as "easier" work, it is assumed that the role is not taxing and does not require specialized expertise—or a lot of time. I have never seen a successful interim trustee leader. In "10 Ways Boards Screw Up Leadership Transitions," Joan Garry notes that the only thing worse than putting a board member in charge during the transition is to allow that board member to remain on the board while also serving as interim director.[2]

The trustee-turned-interim assumes the salary of the departed leader, which is usually much less than they are accustomed to making, and they therefore consider it a part-time and casual role. Meanwhile, the staff, which generally makes a salary a fraction of the director, resents the trustee, who is making a large salary and seeming to work only part-time.

If the board decides they do not have any leaders in-house who are equipped to carry out interim leadership, there are other alternatives. I have seen great success with hiring retired CEOs from other nonprofits to serve in a temporary capacity. Networking phone calls will quickly source some potential candidates, as well as calls to the sector's membership associations.

ASSEMBLING A SEARCH COMMITTEE

Search committees are often led by the current board chair, a future board chair, or a recent past chair. Usually, the board chair has their hands full being an effective chair during a leadership transition, so I advocate for a former chair or a general trustee who knows the institution well, has served in a variety of capacities, and has some CEO search experience. Whoever is selected, they should be prepared to invest a significant amount of time in the search. If the person who has asked you says, "We can wrap this up quickly, and it won't take a lot of your time," don't believe them! The committee leader needs the "Three Ps"—passion, patience, and political savvy.

The search chair should be a strong leader who is able to build consensus and resolve conflicts when consensus is not possible. This person will need trusted staff support for logistics and scheduling. It is important that they have substantive expertise and experience in the nonprofit's mission, history, and strategic priorities. Ideally, the search chair has participated in other searches and is able to judge leadership and emotional intelligence. The chair should be a great communicator who is prepared to keep the committee and board informed of progress, but is also able to maintain confidentiality. It is likely that the chair may also have to address behavioral issues with a committee member, which can be difficult to do with a peer trustee.

The search chair should be prepared for intense lobbying during the period of the search. It begins with requests for a position on the search committee and moves on to trustee, staff, and stakeholder pet issues they would like the new CEO to address. Cocktail parties will quickly turn to the subject of the search, and gossips will deftly try to solicit information. The chair of the search committee must remain resolute in their decision about committee size and makeup as the pressure for seats will be intense.

Any search consultant will advise that the committee should be small—listen to them! A small committee makes it easier to schedule meetings and to have candid, focused, and substantive discussions. It is also easier to focus on a reasonable number of the most critical skills and experience necessary for the job. The larger the committee, the more likely it is to chase a unicorn. The ideal committee size is five to seven members, and fewer than ten. Careful consideration must be given at the start of the process as to the skills needed to find the right leader at the specific moment in the organization's history. In an ideal world, potential donations should not be the reason someone is included on a search committee—but this situation is often difficult to avoid for nonprofits. If already identified, the future board chair should serve on the committee.

Nonprofit boards frequently feel they need to have significant non-trustee community representation on the search committee. While I understand the impulse, it should be resisted. Community volunteers do not have the fiduciary responsibility of a trustee, they rarely know the institution as well as a trustee, and they may or may not have any expertise in the day-to-day work of the organization, or knowledge of how to hire leaders. A friend recently asked me for advice about applying for a role where 60 percent of the search committee consisted of non-trustee community members. I strongly urged the friend not to apply, as the board's delegation of their primary duty (hiring and firing the CEO) was a warning signal of dysfunction. Community input, however, is important and should rightly occur during the preparation and research phases of the search.

Nonprofit boards understand that a search committee should be both diverse and inclusive. If the board's only way to include people of color on the committee is to include non-trustee community members (i.e., there are no people of color on the board), then the board has a greater problem than filling a search committee and must address their lack of representation. The chair should avoid having a single person on the committee to represent diversity (gender, age, race, sexual preference, disability, etc.). The search committee chair must also be studiously attuned to the dynamics of representation on the committee. For example, the committee must not consider the only role of people of color on the committee as being to provide diversity expertise. Doing so simply racializes them and assumes a kind of "universal experience."[3] It should be clear that all members of the committee are equally responsible for championing all forms of diversity. The search committee is the board's proxy to candidates who will perceive the institution's inclusiveness by the committee's makeup and behavior. A diverse and inclusive committee, therefore, will help to attract great candidates and sell the organization.

Filling a committee with donors because you want their funding, community advocates because you want the community to feel buy-in, and elected officials because you want to lobby them are all the wrong reasons to put someone on a search committee. Those relationships are important, and they can be served thoughtfully in the search preparation and the new CEO onboarding. But to delegate the board's most important responsibility to non-fiduciary outsiders is a recipe for failure.

Staff should never have a seat on the search committee. It is a conflict of interest for staff to select their own boss, it makes confidentiality more difficult, and it can make it harder to have candid conversations about the institution's challenges with potential candidates. The incumbent leader should never serve on the search committee for their replacement. While their advice can be sought judiciously and sincerely at certain parts of a search, they should not have any meaningful involvement in the search itself.

Filling the search committee with the wrong people makes it more likely the organization will hire the wrong leader.

TRUSTEE DYNAMICS

The search process is sometimes the first time the board is brought in to "look under the hood." It is not uncommon that trustees learn about issues of which they were not aware. These discoveries embarrass them, they don't want to "air their dirty laundry," and they don't want the outgoing leader to look bad. It can be a humbling experience for boards.

Search committees are often filled with alpha-leaning individuals, many of them accustomed to making independent decisions in their work lives. In this context, they must learn how to work in a group of people without a formal hierarchy (i.e., they are not employees or subordinates). Search hiccups can occur because the committee has interpersonal issues that they must get out of the way and that may have little to do with the search. Committee members with outsize influence—usually financial—can derail a search and leave committee members feeling unempowered. A good search consultant is also a group facilitator, and they will help the committee resolve some of these interpersonal issues, but the heavy lift is for the committee chair.

Search firms will give committee members marketplace feedback, which is helpful not only in the search but also for the board. It is not uncommon that the board is the problem. Candidates want to know if the board understands the job of a trustee and if the governance of the institution is healthy. Most importantly, they want to know if trustees are as financially supportive as the aspirations of the institution require. Because trustees are part-time volunteers who drop in and out of an organization, they are sometimes not fully aware of board dysfunctions. A good search consultant can help advise the board on governance issues to resolve before the new leader begins, but the board must be strong enough to hear it and committed enough to fix things. Boards are quick to celebrate how hard-working and dedicated the board is and equally quick to dismiss problems in their midst. The best gift they can give to their new leader is to fix governance problems, including problematic trustees, before the new CEO arrives. It takes courage for trustees to face up to their peers.

CONFIDENTIALITY

Confidentiality is one of the most important—and difficult—qualities that must be maintained in a search committee. For the process to be fair and efficient, the conversations and actions of the committee have to be kept confidential. It is also critical for potential applicants that their candidacy be kept confidential, as a leak could jeopardize their current employment and reputation. The search committee chair should think twice about putting someone who trades in gossip on the committee. Committee members should be asked to sign a nondisclosure agreement, and ideally, one that states that failure to adhere to the policy will lead to removal from the committee and possibly from the board of trustees. I am aware of several searches that failed to secure their preferred candidate because of violations of confidentiality.

FIXIN' TO SEARCH

Another favorite Southern phrase of mine is "fixin' to," as in "I am thinking about, planning for, and preparing to eventually do something." If you are thinking about the time when you might prepare to leave your house, you are "fixin' to get to going." An important part of a leadership search is all the advance work that needs to happen before the search even begins. It's human nature that the day when a CEO announces their planned departure, trustees rush to begin the transition, with promises to staff and board that the search will be conducted quickly and wrapped up in a matter of months. In fact, with a good interim leader identified, the board should not feel rushed.

In his book, *Chief Executive Transitions: How to Hire and Support a Non-Profit CEO*, Don Tebbe identifies six types of transitions. [4] Tebbe notes that understanding which type of transition the organization faces will help the board to determine what kind of leader they need next—for not all searches are the same. Tebbe's six classic transition types are:

1. Sustained success:

    This type of organization is performing well, and the board says, "Just don't screw it up." The incumbent CEO is a respected leader, the staff is high-functioning, and the organization is making major achievements in serving its mission.
2. Underperforming:

    The organization appears to be in decline and is not meeting its potential. The institution feels stale and uninspiring. Trustees, staff, and funders lack the energy that comes from sustained success.
3. Turnaround:

    A turnaround situation can occur as the result of a crisis (criminal, financial, reputational, etc.) or failed organizational performance. Some stakeholders are likely concerned about the institution's long-term viability.
4. Hard-to-follow executive:

    A long-term charismatic leader who has become universally identified with the organization and maintains broad and deep relationships with stakeholders, donors, and the community. People fear the organization will fold without this leader in place.
5. First hire:

    The first paid professional CEO of an organization, either because it is a startup or because it has historically been volunteer-led.
6. Internal promotion without a search:[5]

    Equipped with a strong succession plan, the board is poised to hire an internal candidate without needing to conduct a search.

Throughout my career, I have heard the same comment from every leader I know who has transitioned to a new nonprofit CEO position: "The board never told me the full story." Part of this response is just naivete—of course, the board doesn't know the complete picture of an organization. But at its heart, it reflects the board's lack of preparation for a new CEO. This is also true of the for-profit world, where "close to 50 percent of chief executives say that the role was 'not what I expected beforehand.'"[6] The problem isn't always ignorance on the part of the boards; they are also sometimes reluctant to "air the dirty linen." They are concerned about how poorly they will look individually if the state of the organization is revealed to others. Just like home inspectors, boards should disclose any known significant problems to candidates before making an offer.

THINKING AHEAD

Bruce Feiler's book, *Life Is in the Transitions*, is about the impact of life transitions on individuals, but his points are also true of organizations.[7] A major transition is an opportunity for the board to take stock of the organization at that point in time. It is also a time to consider a dynamic and changing world and anticipate challenges the new CEO might face in the next three to six years.

The era of ten-year "long-range plans" is over, but hopefully the institution has an effective and current strategic plan, complete with a powerful mission and vision and an explicit values statement. This document should be the starting point for the board's planning. This is a great moment to create some focused board and community task forces, which involve the stakeholders in the search, and enable them to learn more about the institution firsthand. Task forces could include talent strategy, financial analysis, facility analysis, fundraising capacity, audience, community engagement, and public service review.

Another excellent approach is to engage a consultant to help with some pre-search introspection. An analysis of current strengths, weaknesses, opportunities, and threats (SWOT) can help determine the organization's strategic priorities and envision future priorities. The goal is to help the board see the true health of the organization and anticipate major obstacles and challenges the new leader will encounter. They will identify core structural, programmatic, and talent challenges a new leader will face, thereby offering the board insight into the skills and experience needed in the new leader.

This information will help to focus the search committee's work on candidates who are most appropriate to tackle the challenges and opportunities ahead. In the absence of this direction, search committees often look for someone who is most able to keep the organization in its current position. This work will also provide prospective candidates with insights and information that will help them in decision-making about the opportunity. It is much better to be transparent about the "warts and all" institutional picture so that the board finds a candidate who is informed and up for the challenge.

THE BODIES IN THE BASEMENT

"We will just leave that for the new director to fix" is the go-to solution for organizations in transition. Trustees and staff members rely on this pass-the-buck strategy, and both small and large problems are ignored and gleefully left for the new director to resolve. From personnel problems to legal issues, staff and trustees delight in delegating responsibility to the as-yet-to-be-hired new CEO. I once inherited a literal body stashed in the basement—an allegedly ancient Chinese burial suit made of jade plaques to encase the deceased. A promised gift to the museum, of questionable provenance and authenticity, it was left lying on a large table, under a sheet, in the storage vault. Because that hot, human-sized potato was left for the new director, and the owner of the object didn't like the way that I resolved it, I had to start my tenure by upsetting (and losing) a patron of the museum. For the remaining eight years of my tenure, this patron wouldn't speak to me. If the board had addressed it before my arrival, we could have started with a clean slate and formed a relationship helpful to the museum.

Don Tebbe refers to this as "savior thinking," noting that instead of dealing with "legacy issues, the board pins all of its hopes on the talent of the incoming executive." These issues can be behavioral, systemic, structural, governance, and financial. Not resolving them during the interim period can delay and handicap the new leader.[8] During this transition period, the board should be courageous and work with the outgoing director and/or the interim director to resolve some of these legacy issues before the new CEO arrives.

EXTERNAL

Part of the pre-search preparation work might also consider societal change and the external factors the new CEO might face during their tenure. Attention should be given to potential external threats and disruptors, locally, nationally, and globally. Trustees could consider the potential impacts of the economy, political climate, public discourse, technological factors, demographic trends, etc. External events could threaten or help the institution in the years ahead, and an understanding of the opportunities and threats should impact the type of leadership an organization needs at this time.

For example, I would not advocate for the appointment today of any leader who does not have a strong understanding of climate change and the possible implications of this crisis on the organization. Likewise, they should be able to discuss the possible impact of artificial intelligence on their industry in the short and medium term. They do not have to be experts in these areas, but they should be educated and articulate about how their sector will be impacted by imminent threats and opportunities. A candidate who is not thoughtful about looming massive global issues and crises should be disqualified, as it shows they have little external awareness or ability to perceive and anticipate likely threats and opportunities.

The "fixin' to" phase offers many benefits: the board can align strategic priorities to the skills and traits of potential future leaders; it is a good bonding time for trustees; potential candidates will gain a better understanding of the challenges and opportunities of the job as they make their decisions; and the new leader can hit the ground running after they arrive.

HIRING A SEARCH FIRM

I am a huge fan of working with search consultants. The money you spend will come back to you in a good hire and a professional search experience. Hiring a search firm is one of the easiest parts of the search process. There are likely to be several qualified firms who work in your nonprofit's industry. A few calls in the CEO's and trustees' networks will source some good firms who will be happy to send proposals to the chair of the search committee. The hiring selection will largely be made based on chemistry with the consultants, as well as their relevant experience in the market, as pricing is generally similar. Large firms will have multiple services they can add to the contract, including organizational culture fit analysis, leadership capability assessments, psychometric analyses, cultural competency surveys, compensation benchmarking, etc.

It is important to understand what a search firm can and cannot do for you. While they will interview stakeholders and draft the position description for review based on your input, their work is only as good as the information you provide. If the board does a good job in the "fixin' to" phase, providing a current strategic plan and/or an institutional assessment document, the work of the consultant will be stronger. It is also important to build in enough time with the staff, in small groups, one-on-one, and with the ability to send email input. Boards should resist the urge to only engage senior leadership, as staff across the organization will have excellent input. In the museum world, if the security guards are disgruntled, you can learn a lot about the health of the museum by listening to them. Board members rarely know in detail what the organization's internal challenges are, and staff can be hesitant to tell them. They will, however, often provide excellent and candid feedback to strangers, such as search consultants. Search consultants will usually also include community stakeholders and industry leaders in their informational interviews before going into the market.

In my field, museum director position descriptions look much the same. Often, boards write them for their assurance that they have adequately described the unicorn they seek. Nobody can blame them for leaving a single quality or expected experience off the list. The committee should support them, however, helping them to be more focused on creating a position description that describes the great challenge and opportunity the organization faces at this point. The document should reflect the weight of the most important candidate qualities they seek to meet those challenges.

In "10 Ways Boards Screw Up Leadership Transitions," Joan Garry clearly describes common problems in nonprofit searches. In describing the position description, she writes facetiously, "Be sure it is comprehensive so that no living being with the exception of the Messiah will have the requisite skills and attributes. . . . "[9] Garry notes how many months are wasted on creating a job description that includes every single suggestion made by committee members, board members, donors, staff, volunteers, and community members. Our desire to be inclusive leads us to feel that all suggestions and priorities must be somehow reflected in the position description.

Ram Charan argues that in seeking a CEO, board members should understand both the current and future capabilities that are critical for the organization's success: "The result is not a laundry list of leadership traits any CEO should have, nor is it a single item. It's a strand of two or three capabilities that are tightly interwoven and required for the new leader to succeed."[10]

Charan describes the work boards need to do before starting the CEO search to understand the current challenges of the industry and how our quickly changing world might further impact the organization's future. These boards embark on expansive research of both the internal and external context impacting the industry. Charan writes, "They don't dismiss complexities or contradictions; they cut through them and deduce what skills and capabilities are essential, iterating until they hit on the right combination."[11] He cites the specific example of IBM's search for a new CEO in 1993. The industry assumed that technological skills were the most important qualification for the job. Through their intensive research about the company's problems, the board decided they needed to pivot and hire for "a mix of proven business acumen, customer orientation, and the ability to make a large organization more decisive and accountable."[12] IBM ultimately hired Lou Gerstner, "a marketing whiz" who was able to diagnose IBM's problems.

Nonprofit boards tend to be conservative. Unless the departing CEO was a failure, they are often more comfortable seeking continuity than change. Boards should resist the known comfort of continuity and study the organization's needs so they can be ready to surge toward an even brighter future for the organization.

COMPENSATION PLAN

Concurrent with the search, the board should initiate a compensation study for the new executive. Boards frequently make assumptions about compensation, such as "we can pay them what the former CEO made, they were happy enough" or "the former CEO was here for decades, so we should offer a lower salary for someone new." To attract talent, you must have a competitive compensation package in the industry. Some search firms can do benchmarking studies for you, and there are a number of nonprofit compensation consultants who can also help. Alternatively, a committee of the board can do their own research, accessing GuideStar, industry associations, and other benchmarking surveys. Whatever strategy you use, take it seriously and make sure you have a competitive package. Once you have hired your CEO, do not forget to benchmark their compensation against comparable institutions at least every two to three years.

NOTES

1. George Bradt, "What Harvard Must Do to Onboard Its New President Successfully," *Forbes*, February 2, 2024, https://www.forbes.com/sites/georgebradt/2024/02/02/what-harvard-must-do-to-onboard-its-new-president-successfully/.
2. Joan Garry, "10 Ways Boards Screw up Leadership Transitions," Joan Garry Consulting, June 27, 2022, https://www.joangarry.com/leadership-transitions/.
3. Özlem Sensoy and Robin DiAngelo, "'We are all for diversity, but . . .' How Faculty Hiring Committees Reproduce Whiteness and Practical Suggestions for How They Can Change," *Harvard Educational Review* Vol. 87, No. 4 (Winter 2017), https://doi.org/10.17763/1943-5045-87.4.557.
4. Don Tebbe, *Chief Executive Transitions: How to Hire and Support a Nonprofit CEO* (Washington, D.C.: BoardSource, 2008) 27–34.
5. Tebbe, *Chief Executive Transitions*, 27–34.
6. Neal H. Kissel and Patrick Foley, "The 3 Challenges Every New CEO Faces," *Harvard Business Review*, January 23, 2019, https://hbr.org/2019/01/the-3-challenges-every-new-ceo-faces.
7. Feiler, *Life is in the Transitions*, 147–49.
8. Tebbe, *Chief Executive Transitions*, 18.
9. Garry, "10 Ways Boards Screw up Leadership Transitions."
10. Ram Charan, "The Secrets of Great CEO Selection," *Harvard Business Review*, November 14, 2016, https://hbr.org/2016/12/the-secrets-of-great-ceo-selection.
11. Charan, "The Secrets of Great CEO Selection."
12. Charan, "The Secrets of Great CEO Selection."

4

The Selection

Nothing good comes of having the wrong CEO. —Ram Charan, *The Secrets of Great CEO Selection*[1]

Equipped with an intriguing position description, agreement on the most important qualities in a candidate, a small and engaged search committee, and perhaps a search consultant, the organization is ready to move from "fixin' to" search to the actual search. Strap in!

As I introduced in chapter 1, you should be in the ABR mindset (always be recruiting). If you are always looking for talent, you have an antenna that seeks to find talented people across many spheres of your life, even when you are not actively looking to fill a particular vacancy. My antenna is always switched on in ABR mode, enabling me to keep a packed Rolodex of talented people. I am often able to make surprising hires because I track people for their emotional intelligence, skills, intelligence, and leadership qualities. When I have a vacancy, I may approach someone who lacks specific experience for a certain job but has all the qualities for success.

For example, I observed the excellent way a waiter with one of the catering companies that a museum used for special events looked after our museum patrons. When we had an opening for the deputy head of visitor services, I urged the hiring manager to consider him for the opportunity, even though the gentleman had never worked in a museum or held a customer service representative position. He did a marvelous job in this new role because he had the qualities we needed. While it was not my responsibility to recruit for this hire, because I practice ABR, I am sometimes able to make successful matches, as in this case.

I learned about searching for candidates in new forums from Robert Stephens, the founder of the Geek Squad. As the Geek Squad started to take off, Robert needed to hire a lot of talent quickly. He decided to go right to the source to find places where "geeks" congregate. Stephens sponsored science-fiction film festivals in the region, with the caveat that he could speak before the films, where he would describe his new company and encourage tech geeks to apply. If you need a geek, go to where the geeks are; don't just expect them to find you.

Similarly, in 2004, Google placed an anonymous billboard on Highway 101 with a puzzle to be solved online. When participants arrived at the site, they found another puzzle. People who successfully solved both puzzles were invited to apply for jobs at Google. Eric Schmidt, Google's CEO from 2001 to 2011, said, "We run this company on questions, not answers."[2]

THE INTERVIEW: CEO CANDIDATE

In the *New Leader's 100-Day Action Plan*, the authors describe interviews as "exercises in solution selling."[3] They argue that all interview questions are just a subset of three questions. To ace the interview, think about situations, actions, and results that will confirm these three questions, which are:

1. What are your strengths (i.e., can you do the job)?
2. Will you love the job (i.e., will you be motivated)?
3. Can we tolerate working with you?[4]

Years ago, when on the interview circuit, I kept an interview notebook in which I listed the questions I expected to be asked in the interview and bullet points with potential answers. It's not hard to figure out many of the questions you will likely be asked. Before the interview, I would review my outline. Immediately after the interview, usually at the airport on my way home, I would write down all the questions I was asked and record my answers (followed immediately by handwritten thank-you notes). The interview notebook became my cumulative preparation for all interviews. Interviewing is "game day," and the candidate must not only prepare intellectually, but also emotionally. I found my interview notebook was the ideal way to focus both thoughts and emotions during my preparations.

Interviews are such artificial environments; it can be difficult to figure out how to approach the room. Almost everyone is nervous at first, and the start of the interview is usually particularly awkward. Hopefully, the committee throws a softball question to warm everyone up. I find that as candidates struggle to find their groove, they have the tendency to be long-winded during the first question, which starts things off on the wrong foot. Keep your responses tight; you want to answer the question, but not ramble. Never stop reading the room; you can usually tell if you are talking too much or too little.

You want to convince the committee of your competence, experience, and skills to perform the tasks, but if they have invited you for an interview, they probably already have this information. Try to construct your comments so that you show confidence checked by humility; always admit what you don't know and tell them how you would get up to speed. Have an opinion, but don't be opinionated. You also want to come across as authentic and passionate about your profession. Think of elegant ways to work in all the research you have done about the organization in advance. Focus on accomplishments, not tasks. You should be able to inspire the committee with your belief in the change the nonprofit can make.

Remember that leadership interviews are generally behavioral interviews; the committee wants to know how you handled past situations, as past behavior can be a good indicator of future behavior. They will want to hear details and to know *your* role in the successful project you describe. As you prepare for the interview, consider what is known in the interview world as the STARR method: Situation (give the context); Task (share the specific task or goal you took on); Action (tell what actions you took); Result (confirm how it went); and Reflection (share what you learned).[5] As you prepare for your interview, think about some of the usual interview questions (tell me how you resolved a difficult HR issue; tell me how you led a change initiative, etc.) and map your responses using the STARR method. Interviewing committees will want to hear specifics, so avoid generalizations and be clear about your specific actions, avoiding the use of "we did. . . . " Resist the temptation to ramble, and stick to the question at hand.[6]

Do not blow your opportunity when asked at the end, "Do you have any questions for us?" Remember that this is probably not about you getting information from them, but having another opportunity to communicate how astute and thoughtful you are. They want to hear that you are curious and interested in the job. It is usually your opportunity to leave a lasting impression. Avoid the usual questions, such as "What kind of candidate are you looking for?"; "What are the next steps?"; and "How committed is the board?" These standard questions aren't necessarily harmful, but they don't cause you to stand out due to your research and perceptiveness. Never decline the opportunity to ask a question unless you have already decided that you do not want the job. GE's Jeff Immelt has pointed out that you don't get a job because of what you know; you get it based on how fast you can learn and internalize what you learn.[7]

At the end of the best interview of my life, I got a standing ovation from the search committee, and I left feeling I had aced the interview questions and developed a rapport with the board members. To my surprise, I didn't get the job. It is human nature that when we don't win the prize in a job search, we think it is an indictment of us, our background, or how we did in the interview. I always advise candidates who feel discouraged at these times to remember that they don't know who their competition was and what exactly the committee was looking for. It's easier said than done, but don't take rejection personally; it may have little to do with you and everything to do with someone else.

Once you have been made the job offer, you will probably want to do some additional research. Institutions are more willing to share information with their prospective leader than with a candidate. Kimerly Rorschach, former director of the Seattle Art Museum, wrote an excellent list of topics and questions a candidate can consider before accepting a job. *Know Before You Go* includes specific questions around a range of topics, including finance, staffing, governance, legal issues, etc., which can help a candidate make an informed decision about making the move.[8] Although the list was written for art museum professionals, it is largely applicable to other nonprofit fields.

THE INTERVIEW: COMMITTEE

Interviews are an imperfect exercise, but they serve many purposes. One should always be conscious of the artificial environment of the interview and create additional opportunities to see a candidate in action. I always include a meal of some sort with all the candidates I see for roles reporting to me. The social setting and implied intimacy of dining together enables a different kind of rapport to develop. Candidates frequently let down their guard, and you learn more about them as people. I keenly watch for clues, such as the way they treat waitstaff.

I once courted a highly qualified curator as a potential candidate for a vacancy and visited him at the large museum he was serving at the time. As we walked through the galleries on our way to and from lunch, I noticed that he completely ignored his colleagues in security, even though we were often the only people in the room. As we moved through the galleries, he was eager to show me artwork he had acquired, but he didn't smile or greet a single security officer; it was as though they just didn't exist. Due to the way he treated his colleagues, I decided not to pursue the appointment. Committees should watch how the candidate meets people and how they engage the receptionist and other office staff they encounter. Read every signal and sign you are offered.

There are many ways to conduct the formal interview portion of the search. I have seen committees develop a focused list of questions they ask each and every applicant, with questions assigned to specific committee members. In one unusual interview, the head of the search committee, a litigator, fired away all the questions, and committee members were merely observers. I don't recommend this approach.

More often, interviews are freeform, and members ask questions across a broad spectrum, as thoughts come to them. This is an inefficient use of everyone's time, as committee members can become distracted and chase down rabbit holes. I have seen search committees waste time with functional questions, like "How often does your museum offer free days?" When committee chairs see this happening, they need to refocus the committee members on agreed-upon lines of inquiry, with a specific understanding of what they are trying to learn about the candidate.

Although it is more time-consuming, I am an advocate for interviews where committee members meet with candidates in very small groups (two to three people), in addition to the formal group interview. It can be grueling for the candidate, but this approach can surface more information than the group setting. As each team pursues different lines of questions, they can then come back and compare notes to assess the primary qualities they are looking for, as evidenced by different lines of questions.

Boards are often looking for someone who has already done the exact job for which they are hiring. I understand the impulse; it feels much riskier to take a bet on someone who has not performed all the functions of the job and at the same scale. When I directed a small museum earlier in my career, I constantly received calls from search consultants asking me to apply for similar small museums—very clearly a lateral move for me. Sometimes, people choose lateral moves for personal reasons, like proximity to family. Excepting personal reasons, I always felt these boards shouldn't want me for a lateral or down-ward move, as it could indicate a lack of success in the current role and/or a lack of drive and ambition to achieve big goals. In general, institutions should want someone on their way up, not on their way back down. In these cases, I fear the egos of trustees get in their way. Boards would sometimes rather announce that they secured a candidate from a similar or more prestigious institution than that they are investing in new talent.

If a committee is not easily finding someone who has adequately already done the job, how do they interview and analyze a candidate who has not performed this specific job, at the same scale and complexity in the past? Having done all the work in the "fixin' to" search phase, the committee is equipped with an understanding of the key qualities they are looking for to navigate the three to four greatest challenges and opportunities facing the organization.

In his article on hiring talent, Ram Charan notes that nobody is perfect, and every CEO has areas where they are not as strong and he urges boards to "plan for imperfection" and be prepared for trade-offs.[9] Part of the interview process is to confirm that the candidate is self-aware and knows where they might need some help. On multiple occasions, I have asked candidates to describe areas with which they might need additional help. More often than not, the candidate announces that they don't need any help or picks something self-evident, like "scheduling." In one instance, I even suggested to the candidate who didn't think they had any weak areas that perhaps humility could be help-ful. They were not self-aware enough to accept the invitation to think about the question differently. I would hazard that anyone presenting themselves as per-fect will probably not be a successful leadership candidate. In another instance, a candidate told me that their area of weakness occurred when people didn't appreciate and adore them enough. Neither of these people moved forward in their searches.

Rather than pursue the unicorn, boards should recognize that there are multiple ways to fill in any gaps in a leading candidate. Working with coaches or consultants or hiring additional expertise in-house can help to round out gaps in knowledge and experience.

While serving as director of the Minneapolis Institute of Art (Mia), I had the good fortune of working with the visionary philanthropist Bruce B. Dayton. Dayton, who passed away in 2015 at the age of ninety-seven, had served as a trustee and emeritus trustee for seventy-four years. I often thought about all Bruce had seen of the museum's growth and change during those seventy-four years. He once said to me, "You're doing a good job. You are not the best director we have ever had, but you are second best." I learned that his "best director" had died before I was even born.

When Bruce first joined Mia's board in the 1940s, the museum was relatively small and focused almost exclusively on growth. Leaders were judged by how many great works of art were added to the collection and how many additional square feet were constructed. The job of the museum was to purchase a work of art and hang it on the walls. Now museums have large staffs that research, insure, raise funds, photograph, interpret, catalog, and create digital information about every work that comes into the building. Over Bruce's tenure, the museum increased exponentially, from its physical size to increases in staffing, budget, stakeholders, programming, and operations. The museum, and others like it, have become large and complex organizations, still emphasizing growth, but also community participation and impact, and they exist in a complex world.

When Bruce joined the board, gentleman scholars (they were almost all male) were hired as directors and expected to sit in their offices and think great thoughts about art. In the museum's archives, I reviewed the daily schedules of the director of Mia when Bruce joined the board. The pages were largely blank, except for a few luncheons each month, regular trustee meetings, and annual buying trips to Europe. Although nobody else had Bruce's tenure, there was still a long institutional memory of this earlier age and only a basic understanding of the work of a museum director in the twenty-first century. Few trustees could see the ways in which the role of the institution and its leader had changed so profoundly in the last twenty-five years.

In addition to the growth in size and scope of nonprofits, our external world is constantly changing. While change is a constant across time, the current pace of change in a global and connected world is exponentially faster, and the external world in which nonprofits now operate is different from ten years ago, let alone forty years ago. Boards, which may understand how the changing external environment impacts their own business decisions, are often not familiar with the impact on a nonprofit's sector. Museums tend to be highly conservative institutions and have proven detrimentally slow to change. For example, census data has long been available to show that American demographics have been changing quickly, telling us that the nation would soon become majority Black, Indigenous, People of Color (BIPOC).[10] Most museum leaders (me included) ignored this information until major foundations held us accountable for diversifying our staffs, boards, and audiences. We are all playing catch-up now, but the information was there all along. Today's nonprofit leader needs to be cognizant of societal changes that will impact their institution in the short and medium term.

I always ask leadership candidates to make a twenty-minute presentation in the second round of interviews. You want to see how well they organize information and communicate. It is a time to gauge their ability to develop and articulate a compelling strategy and align the organization. The person with a fifty-slide PowerPoint deck clearly has not learned to how synthesize and communicate simple and salient points.

> Simplifying the complex is the CEO's job . . . they are paid to create order out of chaos, to identify the three or five things the employees need to focus on.
> —Adam Bryant, *The Corner Office*[11]

Listen for specific topics, such as how they might assemble and motivate a leadership team, and how they would work with the board and external stakeholders. What process would they use to determine resource allocation and understand the organization's talent pool? At the end of the presentation, do you feel inspired to break out your checkbook and step up to support this person?

Do not forget that they are not insiders and they do not have all the information you have about the organization, so do not judge them too heavily on the specific content of the presentation. The goal is to see how well they can inspire with big ideas, concise communication, and practice clear and critical thinking, not whether all the ideas presented could actually be acted upon.

THE CANDIDATE: SHOULD I STAY, OR SHOULD I GO?

Participating in a leadership search can be exciting and energizing for the candidate. The process helps candidates understand themselves and their career goals better and imagine a new kind of future that offers growth and opportunities. It is also exhausting; it takes a lot of time, and one feels guilty sneaking around and "flirting" with another organization. It can feel schizophrenic as you try to juggle your day job with the work of preparing presentations for the search committee. And there is also the anxiety that current trustees, patrons, and staff might hear the rumor that you are interviewing.

As it appears more and more likely that you are going to be offered the job, you should be thinking seriously about the opportunity and what it will mean for your family, especially if a move is involved. We tend to focus on the excitement part until an offer is extended, and then the reality of the change sets in with a *thud*. Early on, be rigorous in asking yourself how much you want the job and why. Can you see yourself in the role, being happy, challenged, and energized? How does the relationship with the board feel? Do you have a rapport with them, and do they have a rapport with each other? How committed are they? Are there any governance problems you can discern? Are there any red flags you are trying not to think about? Can you succeed in the way you would want to succeed? What makes you think so? Will your family be happy in the community? Is the institution in crisis? Will you be able to keep learning? Will this position open even more opportunities for you in the future? Will the position enlarge or reduce you?

You should also be prepared for the offer by doing your research and reviewing salary information in the public 990. Tap your network and find out what others are making in institutions of similar size and other nonprofits in the region. If you are a woman and/or a person of color, ensure that you are compensated fairly. Sadly, women and people of color are still paid less than their white male counterparts (there are countless studies on this topic, such as those conducted by GAO, Center for American Progress, Finely et al., Sullivan).[12] Hiring officials will always have an explanation, such as the long tenure of the white man who previously held the position, but the truth is that women and people of color will not achieve pay equality until they are paid equally.

In considering a move, calculate any increases or decreases in the cost of living that you would likely encounter with a move. Add in consideration of schools and how that might influence your decision about where to live and related expenses. If you do not already have a lawyer, seek recommendations for a lawyer who could review a contract for you. Tap your network for advice on typical contract structures and benefits in your sector. That is to say, take this time to be informed. If you leave the research until the offer is extended, you may be rushed as urgency increases, and if you decline at the offer stage without very good reasons, you risk burning some bridges.

NOTES

1. Charan, "The Secrets of Great CEO Selection."
2. Francesca Gino, "The Business Case for Curiosity," *Harvard Business Review*, September–October 2018, https://hbr.org/2018/09/the-business-case-for-curiosity.
3. George B. Bradt, Jayme A. Check, and Jorge E. Pedraza, *The New Leader's 100-Day Action Plan: Take Charge, Build Your Team, and Deliver Better Results Faster* (Hoboken: John Wiley & Sons, Inc., 2022), 7–9.
4. Bradt, Check, and Pedraza, *The New Leader's 100-Day Action Plan*, 7–9.

5. Sophia Edelstein, "How to Hire and Interview for a High-Growth Business," *Forbes*, January 17, 2024, https://www.forbes.com/sites/forbesbusinesscouncil/2024/01/17/how-to-hire-and-interview-for-a-high-growth-business/.
6. Robin Rayan, "Ace Your Next Interview Using the STAR Method," *Forbes*, May 5, 2023, https://www.forbes.com/sites/robinryan/2023/05/25/ace-your-next-interview-using-the-star-method/.
7. Thomas J. Neff and James M. Citrin, *You're in Charge—Now What? The Eight-Point Plan* (New York: Three Rivers Press, 2005), 22.
8. Kimerly Rohrschach, "Know Before You Go," Center for Curatorial Leadership, June 1, 2017, https://www.curatorialleadership.org/in-the-field/know-before-you-go/.
9. Charan, "The Secrets of Great CEO Selection."
10. William H. Frey, "The US Will Become 'Minority White' in 2045, Census Projects," Brookings, March 14, 2018, https://www.brookings.edu/articles/the-us-will-become-minority-white-in-2045-census-projects/.
11. Adam Bryant, *The Corner Office* (New York: St. Martin's Griffin, 2011), 56.
12. "Women in the Workforce: The Gender Pay Gap Is Greater for Certain Racial and Ethnic Groups and Varies by Education Level," U.S. Government Accountability Office, December 15, 2022, https://www.gao.gov/products/gao-23-106041; Robin Bleiweis, Jocelyn Frye, Rose Khattar, "Women of Color and the Wage Gap," The Center for American Progress, November 17, 2021, https://www.americanprogress.org/article/women-of-color-and-the-wage-gap/; Andrew Finely, Curtis M. Hall, Amanda Marino, "Negotiation and Executive Gender Pay Gaps in Nonprofit Organizations," *Review of Accounting Studies*, *Claremont McKenna College Robert Day School of Economics and Finance Research Paper No. 338548*, March 11, 2021, https://dx.doi.org/10.2139/ssrn.3385848; Paul Sullivan, "In Philanthropy, Race Is Still a Factor in Who Gets What, Study Shows," *New York Times*, May 1, 2020, https://www.nytimes.com/2020/05/01/your-money/philanthropy-race.html.

5

The Leader

Intellect still matters . . . But across all layers of management, the emphasis has gradually shifted towards softer social skills, such as clear communication, ability to build trust, and willingness to show vulnerability. Executives, including CEOs, need to be comfortable with uncertainty and happy to delegate even the strategic responsibilities they once would have hogged. —*The Economist*[1]

So, if boards must hire not only for subject or discipline expertise but also for leadership, what are the most important nonprofit leadership skills in the twenty-first century and how might boards hire for them? I believe critical thinking; curiosity; emotional intelligence; courage; commitment to diversity, equity, and inclusion; and change management are the most important qualities that a successful nonprofit leader must possess to be successful today. To my dismay, these qualities are often dismissively described as "soft skills" and still sometimes considered as "nice to have" qualities.[2] They are, in fact, the necessary skills of a nonprofit leader today, and I will therefore refer to them as "essential skills."

These essential skills are areas where boards are often unaccustomed to probing during an interview. It is much easier to discuss a candidate's ability to adapt to a new town and their experience in fundraising than it is to question courageous leadership during transformational change. In the Appendix, you will find my "go-to" list of possible interview questions, organized by the qualities I am trying to gauge. Boards should not waste a precious minute of their short interview time on unimportant questions, even if they are more comfortable throwing softball questions. When they waste their time with questions that don't gauge leadership potential, they end up hiring mostly for "chemistry" and likeability. Chemistry is immensely important, but it should not replace leadership potential.

The most common mistake that search committees make in interviewing for a new CEO is to focus most of the attention on technical skills. The people the committee will interview will likely be smart and up-to-date in technical skills and knowledge of their industry. At the level of senior leadership, committees should be looking for character, emotional intelligence, and behavioral strengths. As Marshall Goldsmith points out in *What Got You Here Won't Get You There*, "We all have certain attributes that land us our first job. These are the kind of achievements that go on our résumé. But as we become more successful, those attributes recede into the background—and more subtle attributes come to the fore."[3] In his book, Jim Collins identified that the "good to great" companies prioritized character over "specific educational background, practical skills, specialized knowledge or work experience."[4]

In the past, boards used to work hard to find a leader who would keep them out of any kind of crisis. Now, as boards hire leaders, they must assume that their new CEO will experience multiple crises, both internal and external, during their tenure, given today's operating environment. So, in addition to hiring someone you believe will inspire followers, develop an impactful strategy, and build effective teams, you need to hire a person with the skills to navigate unforeseen crises.

CRITICAL THINKING

Increased complexity has elevated the need for sharp critical thinking skills in a leader. Critical thinking requires the ability to understand a problem at hand and think clearly and rationally about the process of arriving at a solution. To do so, leaders need to be able to analyze and interrogate facts and data and know the questions they should ask to solve the problem. This discipline requires curiosity, comfort with ambiguity, a bias for data, and the ability to ask "what?" and "why?" questions and research solutions. In a data-filled world, the successful leader needs to be able to analyze data relevance. While I am always a proponent of the judicious use of instinct, a critical thinker will approach a decision more systematically, with evidence and data, while watching for assumptions and biases. Critical thinking is about being curious and reflective, checking the impulse to be immediately reactive.

A successful critical thinker will actively interrogate assumptions and decisions for shallow understanding and bias. All humans have inherent biases (see chapter 6), so the importance here is in finding someone who can recognize their own biases and who tests them. A critical thinker will examine unsubstantiated claims and the deployment of selective information for bias. While a critical thinker will rely on experience, they will also push themselves to gather additional evidence and facts, recognizing that leadership is always a learning journey. "Our cognitive biases make us the least objective source in assessing our personal behaviors and our company's performance. Be bold and start asking questions."[5] Critical thinkers can often see opportunity where others do not because they are always checking the status quo. Critical thinking can help in managing ambiguity when one is aware of the limitations of the information they have available at the time.

THE CRITICAL ROLE OF CURIOSITY

Innate curiosity has been shown to be associated with the following eight traits—avid learners, problem solvers, active listeners, self-motivation, high productivity, growth mindset, overachieving, and strong at stakeholder management. —Christopher Frank, Paul Magnone, and Oded Netzer, *Harvard Business Review*[6]

In her influential book, *Mindset: the New Psychology of Success*, psychology professor Carol S. Dweck argues that there are two types of intelligence; a fixed mindset and a growth mindset.[7] Someone with a fixed mindset sees intelligence and talents as fixed and innate assets that cannot be changed. They often avoid challenges out of fear of failure and give up easily, seeing effort as fruitless. A person with a growth mindset thinks that abilities can be learned and values both successes and failures as fruitful lessons. A growth mindset person loves learning and values the effort to get better at things. Dweck sees our mindsets as a continuum, as people fluctuate between the two mindsets; they are not forever fixed.[8] After reading Dweck's book, Microsoft's CEO Satya Nadella announced that he wanted to transform Microsoft from a "know-it-all company" to a "learn-it-all company." He has done so by hiring employees who are motivated by learning and by incorporating learning as a way of working at Microsoft, giving employees space and time to learn, and incorporating data-driven insight into their work.[9]

Curious people tend to ask more open-ended questions and are less prone to confirmation bias. Companies that actively promote curiosity are consistently associated with better business performance.[10] Writing about the success of the consulting firm Ideo, Gino writes that the company "recognizes that most people perform at their best not because they're specialists but because their deep skill is accompanied by an intellectual curiosity that leads them to ask questions, explore, and collaborate."[11]

Successful leaders acknowledge that leadership is a perpetual learning journey, which can be difficult. I learned this lesson from one of my mentors, Hubert Joly, the successful CEO who turned around Best Buy when everyone else expected it to fail. I bristled when Hubert suggested he would help me to work with a coach as I thought it implied inadequacy on my part. Hubert said to me, "I play tennis and I always want to be a better tennis player, so I work with a tennis coach. Why wouldn't I do the same as a leader?" Hubert taught me a lesson in humility and therefore leadership—a good leader always acknowledges they are on a learning journey and demonstrates gratitude for every lesson and helping hand along the way.

Curiosity is linked to humility. The word *humility* comes from the Latin *humilitas*, and definitions include "insignificance," "unimportance," "degradation," "base," "needy," and "submissiveness." Rather than a weakness, humility is, in fact, a great strength that enables a person to learn and to become more attuned to the thoughts and feelings of others. While the quality of humility in leaders is gaining traction today, at least since the Middle Ages, it has been dismissed as a female trait—and therefore a weakness. Some leaders carry the harmful assumption that they must be good at everything and that they are infallible; Carol Dweck refers to this as "CEO Disease."[12]

In *Good to Great*, Jim Collins describes transformational leadership as "Level 5," defined as "an individual who blends extreme personal humility with intense professional will."[13] Collins writes at length about how surprising this observation is and how it contradicts both conventional wisdom and contemporary management theory. I would argue that it may be surprising to men who write contemporary management theory, but it comes as no surprise to women. "I suspect that humility gets a bad rap because it is sometimes linked with subservience or weakness or introversion. Psychological research actually indicates the opposite. Humility is most closely associated with a cluster of highly positive qualities including sincerity, modesty, fairness, truthfulness, unpretentiousness, and authenticity."[14]

A humble person acknowledges the limits of their knowledge and experience and seeks to learn more. I admire a highly successful colleague at another museum who is certain in every meeting to ask a variety of questions of the people in the room. His questions are not meant to confirm decisions he has already made or to put people on the spot, but to really understand the spectrum of possible solutions and reveal new points of view in a situation. His approach sometimes throws off employees because they assume he already knows the answers and is trying to trip them up. They are simply not accustomed to a leader who does more listening and questioning than telling.

> I need to be able to walk out of here this evening and say, "Where was I too closed-minded, or where did I not show the right kind of attitude of growth in my own mind?" If I can get it right, then we're well on our way to having the culture we aspire to. —Satya Nadella, CEO, Microsoft[15]

Empathy and curiosity are also related; curious people tend to be active listeners, and in listening to others, they demonstrate an appreciation for another person's lived experience. Empathy is often considered a less-important "soft skill." Being kind and empathetic does not mean a leader cannot also be tough and decisive—one does not negate the other. The best leaders demonstrate both qualities.

One of the criticisms I've faced over the years is that I'm not aggressive enough or assertive enough, or maybe somehow, because I'm empathetic, it means I'm weak. I totally rebel against that. I refuse to believe that you cannot be both compassionate and strong. —Jacinda Ardern[16]

Jacinda Ardern, the former prime minister of New Zealand, excelled in her handling of the COVID-19 global pandemic in New Zealand because she communicated regularly and was honest about the challenge and the sacrifices she was asking of people. She showed humility and relied on others, admitting when she did not know the answers. Ardern led with her heart, showing compassion, and her head, by listening to the expertise of others.

Part of the reason we do not talk much about empathy as a key leadership quality is that it is often also dismissed as a female trait. Studies find that there are neurobiological quantitative differences in men and women when it comes to both affective and cognitive empathy and how emotional information is processed.[17] In "7 Leadership Lessons Men Can Learn from Women," Tomas Chamorro-Premuzic and Cindy Gallop argue: "If men spent more time trying to win people's hearts and souls, leading with both EQ [a measure of emotional intelligence] and IQ, as opposed to leaning more on the latter, and nurturing a change in beliefs rather than behaviors, they would be better leaders."[18] Being kind and empathic does not mean a leader cannot also be tough and decisive—one does not negate the other. The best leaders demonstrate both qualities.

EMOTIONAL INTELLIGENCE

Oh, would some Power the gift give us
to see ourselves as others see us.

—Robert Burns, *To a Louse*[19]

When sitting on search committees, I frequently hear *emotional intelligence* (variously referred to as both *EQ* and *EI*) listed as the last qualification for a candidate, a sort of "bonus" feature on the list of "soft skills." Emotional intelligence refers to a person's ability to understand and manage their own emotions and those of people around them. Our understanding of emotional intelligence is still young; American psychologists Peter Salavoy and John Mayer coined the term *emotional intelligence* just in 1990. They described EI as "a form of social intelligence that involves the ability to monitor one's own and others' feelings and emotions, to discriminate among them, and to use this information to guide one's thinking and action."[20]

The concept was later introduced into the business world by scientist and author Daniel Goleman, who argued that successful business leaders need to understand the relationship between cognitive thought and emotion. In Goleman's 1995 book, *Emotional Intelligence: Why It Can Matter More Than IQ*, he argues that people with strong EI perform better in the workplace. He stresses that the more senior the leader, the more important it is to have high EI.[21] Goleman breaks emotional intelligence into four categories:

1. Social awareness (perceiving other peoples' emotions)
2. Self-awareness (understanding our emotions and the impact we have on others)
3. Self-management (the ability to manage our emotions)
4. Relationship management (understanding the emotions of others and doing so with empathy)

He further breaks out competencies in each of the categories, such as adaptability, optimism, empathy, conflict management, teamwork, influence, and inspirational leadership.[22]

As early as 1972, Albert Mehrabian introduced a theory that only 7 percent of the meaning of our feelings comes from verbal communication; the rest is expressed through body language, facial expression, tone, and inflection.[23] While scholars debate the exact percentages of how we communicate meaning and emotion (context matters), it is true that we communicate emotions through more than verbal communication.[24] People who practice active listening tend to be better at reading nonverbal cues as part of their listening.

Social scientists debate the percentage of importance of IQ versus EI in an employee's success.[25] Exceptional performance among top managers and senior leaders cannot be explained entirely due to IQ.[26] Robert Emmerling and Daniel Goleman refer to IQ as a "threshold competence."[27] As the field of EI matures, there are also numerous debates about the "dark side" of leaders who manipulate people by preying upon the emotional reactions of followers.[28]

In her research study of five thousand participants, industrial psychologist Tasha Eurich discovered that although most participants described themselves as self-aware, only about 10 to 15 percent actually demonstrated this behavior.[29] Importantly, Eurich observes that as people gain power and experience, they become less self-aware and are more likely to overestimate their skills and abilities.[30] Search committees, therefore, should drill down with candidates to understand how they solicit feedback and work to understand how other people perceive them.

Self-awareness is a key part of emotional intelligence. We have both internal self-awareness (how we perceive ourselves) and external self-awareness (understanding how others perceive us and our impact on other people). The biggest problems arise when there is a large gap between the two.

Barbara Khouri, former CEO of Swatch, has said that leaders often must be actors at work because they need to be so careful and measured about the display of their own emotions.[31] A key part of self-awareness is knowing what your emotional triggers are. For me, it is when people recite ridiculous reasons or unrelated data when trying to convince me of something. I am not annoyed by the thing for which they are advocating, but by the assumption that I am not smart enough to see through the silly rationale they are presenting. It sets me off, and I must work hard to control my response.

The artificiality of interviews means they rarely pose a good forum for observing active listening, emotional restraint, and other aspects of EI. More informal settings, like lunches and coffees with small groups of people, offer greater opportunities for understanding a candidate's EI. In these settings, search committees need to listen for self-awareness, noticing candidates who pause before speaking, who are thoughtful in responding to the question asked, and who can speak elegantly about their own occasional failures and shortcomings. They can also answer the strengths and weaknesses questions without falling back on adages such as, "I am an overachiever."

High EI candidates will listen carefully to questions and understand when there is a nuance. For example, my icebreaker question is always, "Can you tell us briefly how your past experience has prepared you to meet with us today about this opportunity?" Candidates usually speak for far too long (ignoring "briefly") and review their entire professional history, without regard to the question of specific relevance to the current opportunity. Search committees should not only listen for specific answers to questions, but also gauge how the candidate listens and interprets questions, looking for evidence of EI.

A great leader needs to be able to read a room and adapt and pivot according to what they perceive is going on. It's a hard skill to master because it involves extreme multitasking; you are often in the spotlight, and you need to adjust your presentation, your language, and your approach in real time. Reading the room means tuning yourself out and focusing on the verbal and nonverbal cues of others and adjusting your behavior accordingly. People who can do this have a superpower because they can both disarm their audience and make the group feel more empowered and invested in what they have to say.

In the last fifteen years, every candidate I have interviewed has mentioned in some fashion how much they value and practice collaboration. It is striking, however, how few also give credit to colleagues and collaborators when discussing their successes. Instead of taking their dedication to collaboration at face value, it is good to double down, asking for specifics and listening for the recognition of other contributors to success. If we use the definition of *collaboration* as two or more people working together in service of shared goals, we see avenues for different questions: What type of person collaborates most effectively? What roadblocks impede collaboration, and how has this candidate overcome them? What happens when two collaborators have different goals?

COURAGE

If I finish my term in office . . . and have high approval ratings, then I wasted my last years in office. That high approval rating means you don't upset anybody.

High approval rating means you're skiing down the slope and you never fall. Well, you're skiing the baby slope, for goodness' sakes. Go to a steeper slope. You always want to press, and you want to tackle the issues that are unpopular, that nobody else will go after. —Michael Bloomberg, quoted in *The Atlantic*[32]

Courage in leadership takes many forms, but it still means having the fortitude and conviction to do difficult things. Today, we understand that courage requires humility, curiosity, and integrity. Authentic leaders make courageous decisions and accept the successes and failures of these decisions with honesty and transparency. They apologize when necessary and unpack and own the lessons learned from their successes and mistakes. As articulated above by Michael Bloomberg, leaders should keep asking themselves if they are being courageous enough.

The most important tool for a courageous leader is to have a sense of purpose and a deep understanding of their values. In today's volatile and noisy world, leaders often need to make quick and difficult decisions. Doing so equipped with their individual and institutional values (if these values are not similar, the leader is working for the wrong organization) is often the only way to make these decisions. I will always be grateful that early in my career, my uncle told me that great leaders must accept that they will sometimes make decisions that people profoundly dislike. He said, "If you're not making some people mad, you're not doing anything." Courage means going to sleep every night knowing not everyone likes you. As a woman who was raised to believe that "being nice" was a woman's most important attribute, I find this one of the harder parts about leadership.

While leading the Minneapolis Institute of Art, we were approached by Valerie Castile, the mother of Philando Castile, an African American man who was fatally shot by police after he was pulled over for a broken taillight. Ms. Castile owns a large collection of artwork given to her by artists to mark her son's life and the tragedy of his death, and she asked us if we wanted to show some of the collection. After a lot of thought and conversation, we decided to do a small exhibition, which we called *Art and Healing*. Mia's board of trustees was very concerned about the exhibition and emphatically urged me not to do it—a board's job, after all, is to protect the institution and its leadership. The board knew that if the show was not done just right, we risked angering Black community members outraged by Castile's killing, along with our traditional stakeholders, the police, and city leadership.

I trusted the staff to get it right, but I also understood the board's concern. Speaking with my board chair about it, I said, "It is hard because it is *hard*." We both nodded; somehow the acknowledgment of the difficulty boosted my courage and justified action. Staring at my office chair behind my desk, I realized I could not face the staff as the leader of the museum if I took the safe and cowardly route. I also realized I believed so profoundly in the project that this was one of the rare occasions that was worth risking my position. Courageous leadership is rooted in defending core principles, even when the potential costs are extremely high.[33]

Courageous leaders are willing to take risks and do not become incapacitated by the fear of failure. A leader who is an effective risk-taker is someone who excels at critical thinking, asking questions, interrogating assumptions, and understanding possible solutions. A courageous leader holds themselves accountable after making the decision and owns up to errors.[34] Leaders take responsibility for mistakes and give credit to others for successes. Sometimes it is also necessary to change direction mid-course, and it takes courage to do that since you must admit you made a mistake. Jake Wobbrock, cofounder of AnswerDash, says his father taught him that everyone wants to be a hero, but "there's no genuine opportunity to be a hero without the opportunity to be a chump, too. . . . If you embrace them both you maybe see the moment more for what it is and you don't fear it as much, and it allows you to perform a little bit better."

AGILITY AND CHANGE MANAGEMENT

> Leadership . . . is about the embrace of change and inspiring people to brave the unknown. —Bartleby in *The Economist*[35]

In addition to IQ and EQ, businesses are now looking for people with AQ— agility quotient. Even before COVID-19 upturned our world, the Flux Report stated that flux would be the world's operating normal going forward and that 91 percent of future leadership recruiting would be based on a leader's ability to deal with resilience.[36] Today's great leaders are skilled in navigating uncertainty and understanding the threats and opportunities that hide in ambiguity. Asking questions, listening, networking, and expansive curiosity will help a leader develop agility skills. Ultimately, agility is about being an innovative and decisive problem-solver who knows when to pivot. Scott Keller points out that agility is not just about speed, "but also balance, coordination, strength, stamina, and reflexes. Being first isn't solely about being fast."[37]

While leaders need to be good managers, they also need to be able to inspire the staff, board, and stakeholders to chart new waters and take risks. A big vision is critical to leadership, but so is the ability to make it happen. Boards therefore need to hire someone who can inspire and motivate others to embrace change and a bold future. All successful organizations need to have a change agent at the helm, and it is the board's job to support them in this work. In the current VUCA world, the status quo is often the riskiest place to be. As

Lian Davey argues, we often consider the potential risks of radical change, but rarely do we analyze the risks of staying the same.[38]

A great leader never lifts their finger off the "change" button. Obviously, not all change is necessary at once, and a leader's critical thinking skills and leadership team will help to determine the pace, scale, and prioritization of organizational change. The need for an agile and adept change agent is even greater in institutions that are replacing long-serving leadership. As already discussed, change of leadership is the best opportunity in an organization's history to launch necessary change—so hire someone who can do it!

Organizational change can be adaptive and evolving. Improving processes; changing institutional culture; and creating new structures, policies, and workflows are examples of smaller-scale, adaptive change. Transformative change could include introducing a new business, franchise, or satellite location; massive program revision; or facility growth. Both types of change require a leader to communicate clearly and regularly about the opportunity for change, helping stakeholders to understand why the change is necessary. Leaders also must establish the time frame and ultimate scope of the project. They should empower others to own the change, and they need to be sure to establish measures of success.

Change agents also must be courageous leaders because managing change is hard. We have all heard that "nobody likes change." Leaders need to be critical thinkers, analyzing data, seeking additional counsel, and asking a lot of questions. They also understand that fear of loss is deeply rooted in the fear of change.

A leader who is good at change management also embeds and empowers change agents throughout the institution. Senior leaders set the direction and tone, and managers throughout the organization lead the change. Change leadership is about engaging people while also moving along those who are not on board. You always want to have people with different perspectives and diversity of opinion who can challenge leadership when decisions are being made. "Divergent, dissident voices are the key to growth and innovation."[39] But once the decision is made and the meeting ends, everyone must be on board.

DIVERSITY, EQUITY, INCLUSION

A curious leader is often someone who excels at supporting a successful culture of diversity, equity, and inclusion (DEI). They enable and empower a culture of diversity and inclusion. They regularly hire people with diverse backgrounds and a point of view that is different from their own, and in making decisions, they pause to consider whose voice is missing at the table. They seek input and advice outside of their normal "bubble." To be an excellent leader today is to be a leader who understands what it means to lead with diversity, equity, and inclusion as a demonstrable practice.

Leading a diverse and inclusive institution often means doing things differently. A leader cannot just profess to value diversity, hire a chief diversity officer, and then continue to operate the business in the same way. Because this leader is humble and curious, they recognize the value of seeing problems and solutions from many different perspectives. A leader must be able to relate and connect with people very different from themselves. Increasing our own cultural competence is a skill that we all need to develop, and it requires time and commitment.

Championing DEI is not simply the right thing to do; it is also a winning business strategy because the more diverse and inclusive an organization, the better positioned it is for success. I am the leader I am today because I have the privilege of learning constantly; my challenge is not only to learn, but also to change my behavior along the way. In hiring leaders, boards need to drill down and ask real questions about a candidate's DEI successes and failures. No candidate will ever tell you that they are not all-in on DEI, so what exactly does that mean? How do they define DEI? Why is it important? How has DEI influenced their leadership? How have they changed their behavior? What examples can they give of how they changed course after learning from people with different perspectives? What metrics are they currently using to measure DEI success? You can ask candidates to address specific tactics they would use to enhance the leadership pipeline, to hire diverse leaders, to include DEI in performance measurement, and to measure inclusion.

NOTES

1. "Pity the Modern Manager—Burnt-Out, Distracted and Overloaded," *The Economist*, October 24, 2023, https://www.economist.com/business/2023/10/24/pity-the -modern-manager-burnt-out-distracted-and-overloaded.
2. Monique Danao, "11 Essential Soft Skills in 2024 (with Examples)," *Forbes*, April 20, 2023, https://www.forbes.com/advisor/business/soft-skills-examples/.
3. Marshall Goldsmith with Mark Reiter, *What Got You Here Won't Get You There* (London: Profile Books, 2007), 53.
4. Jim Collins, *Good to Great: Why Some Companies Make the Leap . . . and Others Don't* (London: Random House, 2001), 51.
5. Stephynie Malik, "Curiosity: A Leadership Trait That Can Transform Your Business to Achieve Extraordinary Results," *Forbes*, August 26, 2020, https://www.forbes .com/sites/forbescoachescouncil/2020/08/26/curiosity-a-leadership-trait-that -can-transform-your-business-to-achieve-extraordinary-results/.
6. Christopher Frank, Paul Magnone, and Oded Netzer, "How to Evaluate a Job Candidate's Critical Thinking Skills in an Interview," *Harvard Business Review*, September 25, 2023, https://hbr.org/2023/09/how-to-evaluate-a-job-candidates-critical -thinking-skills-in-an-interview.
7. Dweck, *Mindset*, 3–14.
8. Dweck, *Mindset*, 234–37.

9. Jo Sweales, "3 Steps to Introduce a Learn-It-All Culture," Microsoft Blog, published January 10, 2019, https://www.microsoft.com/en-gb/industry/blog/cross-industry/2019/10/01/introduce-learn-it-all-culture/.

10. Gino, "The Business Case for Curiosity."

11. Gino, "The Business Case for Curiosity."

12. Dweck, *Mindset*, 20.

13. Collins, *Good to Great*, 21.

14. Jeff Hyman, "Why Humble Leaders Make the Best Leaders," *Forbes*, October 31, 2018, https://www.forbes.com/sites/jeffhyman/2018/10/31/humility/?sh=70dc72101c80.

15. Nat Levy, "Microsoft CEO Satya Nadella: It's better to be a 'learn-it-all' than a 'know-it-all,'" *Geek Wire*, August 4, 2016, https://www.geekwire.com/2016/microsoft-learn-it-all/.

16. Maureen Dowd, "Lady of the Rings: Jacinda Rules," *New York Times*, September 8, 2018, https://www.nytimes.com/2018/09/08/opinion/sunday/jacinda-ardern-new-zealand-prime-minister.html.

17. Leonardo Christov-Moore, Elizabeth A. Simpson, Gino Coudéb, Kristina Grigaityte, Marco Iacobonia, and Pier Francesco Ferrari, "Empathy: Gender Effects in Brain and Behaviour," *Neuroscience and Biobehavioral Reviews* 46, Pt 4: 604–27, https://doi.org/10.1016/j.neubiorev.2014.09.001.

18. Tomas Chamorro-Premuzic and Cindy Gallop, "7 Leadership Lessons Men Can Learn from Women," *Harvard Business Review*, April 1, 2020, https://hbr.org/2020/04/7-leadership-lessons-men-can-learn-from-women.

19. Robert Burns, "To a Louse," accessed February 25, 2024. https://www.poetry.com/poem/30592/to-a-louse.

20. Peter Salovey and John D. Mayer, "Emotional Intelligence," *Imagination, Cognition and Personality* 9.3 (1989): 185–211, https://doi.org/10.2190/DUGG-P24E-52WK-6CDG.

21. Daniel Goleman, *Emotional Intelligence: Why It Can Matter More Than IQ* (New York: Babtam 1995), xv.

22. Daniel Goleman and Richard Boyatzis, "Emotional Intelligence Has 12 Elements. Which Do You Need to Work On?" *Harvard Business Review*, February 6, 2017, https://hbr.org/2017/02/emotional-intelligence-has-12-elements-which-do-you-need-to-work-on.

23. Albert Mehrabian, *Nonverbal Communication* (New York: Routledge, 1977), https://doi.org/10.4324/9781351308724.

24. David R. Novak, "Killing the Myth That 93% of Communication Is Nonverbal," accessed February 25, 2024, https://davidrnovak.com/writing/article/2020/03/killing-the-myth-that-93-of-communication-is-nonverbal.

25. Robert J. Emmerling and Daniel Goleman, "Emotional Intelligence Issues and Common Misunderstandings," The Consortium for Research on Emotional Intelligence in Organizations, October 2003, https://www.eiconsortium.org/pdf/EI_Issues_And_Common_Misunderstandings.pdf.

26. Lyle M. Spencer Jr. and Signe M. Spencer, *Competence at Work: Models for Superior Performance* (New York: Wiley, 1993); Claudio Fernández-Aráoz, "The Challenge of Hiring Senior Executives," in *The Emotionally Intelligent Workplace: How to Select for,*

Measure, and Improve Emotional Intelligence in Individuals, Groups, and Organizations, ed. Cary Cherniss and Daniel Goleman (New York: Wiley, 2003), 182–208.

27. Emmerling and Goleman, "Emotional Intelligence Issues."
28. Adam Grant, "The Dark Side of Emotional Intelligence," *Atlantic,* January 2, 2014, https://www.theatlantic.com/health/archive/2014/01/the-dark-side-of-emotional-intelligence/282720/.
29. Tasha Eurich, "What Self-Awareness Really Is (and How to Cultivate It)," *Harvard Business Review,* January 4, 2018, https://hbr.org/2018/01/what-self-awareness-really-is-and-how-to-cultivate-it.
30. Eurich, "What Self-Awareness Really Is."
31. Adam Bryant, *The Leap to Leader* (Boston: Harvard Business Review Press, 2023), 186.
32. James Bennet, "The Bloomberg Way," *Atlantic,* November 2012, https://www.theatlantic.com/magazine/archive/2012/11/the-bloomberg-way/309136/.
33. James R. Detert, "What Courageous Leaders Do Differently," *Harvard Business Review,* January 7, 2022, https://hbr.org/2022/01/what-courageous-leaders-do-differently.
34. Quoted in Bryant, *The Leap to Leader,* 201–02.
35. Bartelby, "Would You Rather Be a Manager or a Leader?" *Economist,* October 23, 2023, https://www.economist.com/business/2023/10/23/is-being-a-leader-really-sexier-than-being-a-manager.
36. "The Flux Report: Building a Resilient Workforce in the Face of Flux," Manpower Group, accessed January 24, 2024, https://www.manpowergroup.co.uk/wp-content/uploads/2015/04/The-Flux-Report_whitepaper.pdf.
37. Scott Keller, "Reorganizing to Capture Maximum Value Quickly," McKinsey & Company, February 20, 2018, https://www.mckinsey.com/capabilities/people-and-organizational-performance/our-insights/reorganizing-to-capture-maximum-value-quickly#/.
38. Liane Davey, "The Status Quo Is Risky, Too," *Harvard Business Review,* May 2, 2014, https://hbr.org/2014/05/the-status-quo-is-risky-too.
39. Nilofer Merchant, "Don't Demonize Employees Who Raise Problems," *Harvard Business Review,* January 30, 2020, https://hbr.org/2020/01/dont-demonize-employees-who-raise-problems.

6

The Bias Traps

Bias is the favoring of or predisposition toward something or someone or the discrimination or predisposition against someone or something. It is a fixed conception that is not based on fact or objective judgment. We all have bias; it is part of how humans operate. Our brains are efficient engines, and they take shortcuts by creating convenient categories. While this tendency is functional, it can lead to unintended bias and outright discrimination. Explicit bias tends to be visible, but implicit bias is the kind of bias that affects our thinking and actions but of which we are unaware. Biases often favor people who look like us and/or share a similar background and life experience. People in positions of advantage fail to notice bias because of privilege: "Privilege is when you think something is not a problem because it is not a problem for you personally. If you are part of a group that's being catered to, you believe that's the way it should be."[1]

I believe that when nonprofit search committees gather around the boardroom table at the beginning of a search, they are eager to see candidates who are diverse in every possible way. And then they sometimes systematically rule out diverse candidates due to implicit bias. Because committee members come with good intentions, they do not spend time thinking about how racism, sexism, ableism, and other forms of bias and discrimination might affect their views on potential candidates. I recommend all search committees begin their work with a robust training session on how to recognize the bias they and their colleagues might bring to the search.

The best way to help guard against biased-based hiring decisions is to have a diverse search committee, while recognizing that all people bring certain biases to the hiring process. It is hard to eliminate bias from the hiring process, but the ability to recognize and acknowledge it is part of a high-functioning committee. A committee including people with diverse life experiences and perspectives is better equipped to challenge other committee members' unintended biases and assumptions—and they must have the courage to do so. All committee members can monitor and identify bias as they see it and not assume it is the responsibility of diverse committee members to call the behavior.

Bias begins with the first review of résumés when assumptions are often made.[2] Studies have shown that applicants of color who "whiten" their résumés are more than twice as likely to be called for interviews.[3] Job applicants with names assumed to be African American received fewer calls than other candidates.[4] Names, addresses, universities, fellowships, and previous employers are often reviewed by search committees for indications of gender, race, ethnicity, class, sexuality, age, and disability.

Bias challenges continue in the interview phase when implicit biases are reflected in certain kinds of questions and in the ways that committees interpret candidate responses. Ironically, bias is equal opportunity, and in my experience, women can sometimes demonstrate greater sexism than men. A significant part of the challenge is that committee members may not have been exposed to different leadership styles. In America, visible positions held by elected officials and corporate CEOs are still predominantly occupied by able bodied white men. We are therefore not accustomed to seeing and appreciating the leadership styles demonstrated by diverse leaders.

GENDER BIAS: THE TIES THAT BIND

Hillary Clinton's 2016 campaign for president produced a number of articles with misogynistic descriptions, including "bossy," "shrill," "too ambitious," "too angry," and my personal favorite, "sober momliness."[5] Clinton and most women leaders face what linguist Robin Lakoff first referred to as "the double bind" in trying to fulfill contradictory expectations of women leaders.[6] Writing about Clinton's campaign, linguist and author Deborah Tannen explains, "A double bind means you must obey two commands, but anything you do to fulfill one violates the other. While the requirements of a good leader and a good man are similar, the requirements of a good leader and a good woman are mutually exclusive. A good leader must be tough, but a good woman must not be. A good woman must be self-deprecating, but a good leader must not be."[7]

The double bind means that women leaders are criticized for being bossy when they demonstrate top-down leadership, but if they are not explicitly telling others what to do, they are demure and not doing their job. Ambition is seen as a positive quality in a man, but not in a woman.[8] Being called "nice" is the most frequent compliment I ever hear about women. In fact, I try to avoid it entirely and use more specific words as they apply, such as "kind," "warm," "thoughtful," "compassionate," "generous," "helpful," "interesting," etc.

In interviewing for jobs over the years, I often received the same piece of feedback from recruiters: "The committee is concerned that you don't have gravitas." *Gravitas* was one of the key Roman virtues, along with *pietas*, *dignitas*, and *virtus* (which comes from *vir*, the Latin word for "man"). *Gravitas* signifies heft, seriousness, solemnity, and dignity. It is weighty and replete with importance. I have come to realize it is also an unconscious code for "male," as women are rarely ever described as having gravitas; it is a quality that is always associated with men. The double bind dictates that:

- Leaders must have gravitas.
- Women don't have gravitas.
- Women, therefore, cannot be leaders.[9]

One of the questions I have been asked frequently during job interviews is, "Have you ever fired anyone?" It is a silly question on several levels, especially given my years of successful leadership experience. I am consistently asked this question because I smile and display warmth. The question comes from the double bind that expects women to be "nice" and therefore not capable of the leadership qualities of strength and able to make difficult decisions.

EXECUTIVE PRESENCE

The business world has adopted the new term *executive presence* to describe the personal effect that an executive's presence inspires in other people. Writing in *Forbes*, Gerry Valentine describes it as "your ability to inspire confidence—inspiring confidence in your subordinates that you're the leader they want to follow, inspiring confidence among peers that you're capable and reliable and, most importantly, inspiring confidence among senior leaders that you have the potential for great achievements."[10] According to Valentine, a positive executive presence is found in people who have a vision, good communication and listening skills, strong emotional intelligence, political savvy, and appropriate attire.[11] Sylvia Ann Hewlett, widely recognized as the person who coined the phrase, *executive presence*, defines it as having three attributes: gravitas, strong communication skills, and "the right appearance."[12] I have concerns about this concept as a biased way to hire people who reflect a dominant group's preference, and that, as Inga Bielińska argues, it "promotes homogeneity when today's leaders and employees crave authentic expression."[13] If search committees use this quality as a defining factor, I urge them to clearly define the specific aspects of executive presence for which they are looking and beware of unintended bias.

MODERN SEXISM

Like many forms of bias and discrimination, the definition of *sexism* has morphed and adapted to societal changes. Born in the 1960s, I was raised in a world with "traditional sexism," a system in which society endorsed traditional roles for women and openly denied them opportunities. In my twenties, I had a difficult time deciding what I wanted to do professionally because I saw few women who worked outside the home among family and friends, or in the national public sphere. Long-suffering Mary Tyler Moore was the only fictional professional woman on television in my youth. I just could not picture a working woman because I did not see many. Fifty years later, we have a woman vice president, four women Supreme Court justices, and a woman director of the National Gallery of Art.

Modern sexism generally shows less blatant disregard for women, but it harbors more subtle bias. It denies there is any existing discrimination against women and refutes that women are offered fewer opportunities than men. Modern sexism does not recognize that a primary reason there are so few women in senior political, corporate, and large-scale nonprofit leadership is due to a biased view of women leaders. Sexism can be targeted at women, LGBTQI individuals, and men.

Despite advances, a girl growing up in America or Europe today still sees few senior women executives and leaders. At the time of this writing, less than a third of legislators in Congress are women, and only 10 percent of Fortune 500 companies are run by women—and these numbers are both all-time highs.[14] In previous generations, the dearth of women leaders was directly attributable to traditional sexism, which denied women opportunities outright. Today, we see so few women leaders because leadership is still defined in male terms—in part because there are too few women in visible leadership positions to show what a woman leader looks like. Over the years, several research studies have shown that when men and women are asked to draw or a describe "a leader," they almost always depict a man.[15]

When I joined the American museum profession in the 1990s, only a small percentage of the members of the Association of Art Museum Directors (AAMD) were women. Thirty years later, the percentage of women directors has risen to just over 50 percent.[16] Nevertheless, almost all the largest museums are still run by men, and women earn about 75 percent of what their male colleagues earn.[17] Earlier on, traditional sexism kept women from these positions, but modern sexism keeps them less well paid and makes advancement more difficult for them. And when institutions encounter a crisis, male leaders are often given a pass, while women leaders are judged to be "unqualified."[18]

GLASS CEILING OR LABYRINTH?

About twenty-five years ago, I served as a judge for the Ms. California competition (the state championship for the Ms. America pageant). As a new museum director in Fresno, California, the governor's wife had asked me to serve, and I thought it best to agree. I learned a lot about gender and leadership in America from the experience. At the end of the day, we were not actually looking for the most physically beautiful candidate, as all the contestants were attractive. And we were not looking for the most talented, the brightest, or the most likely to succeed, even though these categories are weighted most heavily in scoring. When it was all over, I realized our job was to select the woman who fulfilled American stereotypes of what it means for a woman to excel.

We had only one candidate who was academically exceptional, a mechanical-engineering student from the University of California, Berkeley. Ultimately, the Berkeley engineer could not win because she was too smart, ambitious, and self-confident. Instead, the jury picked a woman who did not excel in any category: she was not academically motivated, she was weak in the interview portion, and she was not especially talented. A juror asked each contestant, "Hypothetically, who would you rather be, the president or the president's wife?" It became clear that we were looking for the person who wanted to be the wife of a successful man. Americans' predilection for women's supporting roles would be proven twenty years later by Hillary Clinton: "[Hillary] Clinton has generally been most popular when conforming to traditional gender roles (working on women's issues as First Lady, sticking by her husband during the Monica Lewinsky scandal, loyally serving Barack Obama as secretary of state) and least popular when violating them (heading the health-care task force, serving in the Senate, running for president). Being the first female president, needless to say, violates traditional gender roles."[19]

In *Women and the Labyrinth of Leadership*, Eagly and Carli propose that women do not face a glass ceiling as much as a labyrinth, without simple or direct passage.[20] Despite plenty of obstacles and obscure turns, there is ultimately a route to the center. The labyrinth "begins with prejudices that benefit men and penalize women, continues with particular resistance to women's leadership, includes questions of leadership style and authenticity, and—most dramatically for many women—features the challenge of balancing work and family responsibilities."[21] Our male-defined understanding of what leadership looks like frequently blocks women as they navigate the labyrinth. Women struggle to be heard, without being interrupted, subjected to "mansplaining," or witnessing a man receive credit for their ideas. Meanwhile, multiple studies show that leadership traits common to women often produce greater success in organizations than those traditionally associated with men.[22]

THE LEADERSHIP DIFFERENCE

> On some level people perceive every woman as a receptionist. It doesn't matter if she's president; when they want a pen, they are going to ask her for it. She's supposed to do everything for you. —Deborah Tannen[23]

The difference between men's and women's leadership styles and skills has been widely described.[24] These differences are not absolute, and there are plenty of men who share the characteristics of women leaders, and vice versa. Since men have held positions of power in the workplace and in all branches of government much longer than women, their leadership style is equated with leadership.[25] When men do show traits more often associated with women, they are seen as exceptional, balanced, and having it all. But those descriptions are not used for women. For example, Joseph Rost examined 221 definitions of *leadership* from the last century and concludes that leadership has most frequently been described as "rational, management-oriented, male, technocratic, quantitative, cost-driven, hierarchical, short-term, pragmatic and materialistic."[26] Women are more often associated with consensus decision-making, negotiation, seeking counsel, and weighing options with others. Their leadership is considered more collaborative, participatory, warm, empathic, and focused on enabling the success of others. Women leaders are more often humble, are better communicators, are more prone to self-control, and demonstrate pro-social and moral orientation.[27]

The Bem Sex Role Inventory (BSRI) is a psychological instrument used to assess public perception of gender roles. The study asks people to rank the desirability of sixty adjectives that describe gender roles. Anna Fels notes that the study participants associated women with adjectives that describe a relationship to someone else, observing that "giving" is the primary activity that defines femininity (to a child, employee, husband, boss, spouse, etc.).[28] Survey participants identify women with the following traits: yielding, cheerful, compassionate, sympathetic, understanding, sensitive to the needs of others, warm, tender, gullible, loving toward children, etc. In contrast, men are not defined by theirs relationship to others; "one can be masculine in solitary splendor."[29] The BSRI descriptions for men include traits such as self-reliant, having a strong personality, forceful, independent, analytical, assertive, dominant, self-sufficient, and athletic.

Empathy, generosity, and kindness have proven to be among the most important leadership qualities during the 2020 global COVID-19 pandemic.[30] Staff members, working in isolation and under deeply stressful conditions, longed for human contact and kindness. They needed to hear that leadership cared about their personal and professional difficulties. Given that empathic, compassionate, and nurturing behavior is more typically found in women leaders, this crisis was a time for women leaders to shine. It has been widely noted that the countries that managed the best during the pandemic—Germany, New Zealand, Finland, Taiwan, Iceland, and Denmark—all had women leaders.[31]

Supriya Garikipati, a developmental economist at Liverpool University who was involved in a study of the role of gender and COVID-19 leadership, writes that the results "clearly indicate that women leaders reacted more quickly and decisively in the face of potential fatalities."[32] The study, *Leading the Fight Against Covid: Does Gender Really Matter?*, used a 194-country data set (nineteen of which had women leaders), and the authors found that gender did, indeed, matter. When controlling for population, GDP per capita, urban population, state of health care, elderly population, etc., nations led by women experienced far fewer COVID-19 cases and deaths.[33] Women leaders reacted quickly and decisively and were more people-centric in their reactions, taking fewer risks that led to fatalities.[34] Women leaders also communicated more often and with greater empathy.

COMMUNICATION

Linguistics scholar Deborah Tannen first opened my eyes to the different ways men and women communicate, a difference that typically begins in childhood and is learned. Tannen refers to these differences as "linguistic style," or "culturally learned signals by which we not only communicate what we mean but interpret others' meaning and evaluate one another as people."[35] Tannen is clear that neither system is better; they are merely different. Tannen notes that women communicate to make connections, whereas when men speak, they are more concerned with status and hierarchy.[36] In her groundbreaking book *You Just Don't Understand*, Tannen explains that when a woman tells a man about a problem, he rushes to solve the problem for her.[37] The woman feels that she has not been heard because she was expecting understanding and empathy, not a solution. The man thinks he was simply being helpful by offering a solution and doesn't understand the woman's hurt feelings. Problem-solving and hierarchy consciousness are often part of male communication patterns. When a woman tells another woman a problem, her confidant will often respond by commenting that she understands because she has had similar experiences—"I *know*, that happened to me too." Conversation brings them closer through solidarity. In turn, men feel frustrated that women are not discussing the problem to solve it. Men sometimes avoid sharing problems with others because to admit to an unresolved problem is to show vulnerability.[38]

Tannen notes that all communication functions on two levels—message (meaning of the words) and metamessage (meaning of the words spoken in relationship to the conversation).[39] When women discuss a problem, they often create an emotional bond by asking questions and sharing personal experiences. However unintended, cutting a conversation short with a solution can send the metamessage that you do not care about the issue or the speaker.

The need to navigate gender metamessages does not come into play for women as often in the cultural heritage sector because the field has so many women employees. Many of us are busy with what Tannen calls "troubles talk."[40] It comes into play, however, when women leaders are immersed in predominantly male environments, like the boardroom or the corporate C-suite. Anticipating gender metamessages is important when women are interviewing for leadership jobs. In this setting, male conversation patterns often dominate, and women should be adept at navigating male conversations. For example, nonprofit CEO candidates are often asked by a search committee, "How much of your time do you spend fundraising?" At first, I would spend my time talking at length about relationship development, donor cultivation, and always being "on" as a public figure. I am still selling when I run into a patron in the frozen food section of the local grocery store on a Saturday morning. Someone eventually took me aside and let me know that men are just looking for a specific solution and don't want to hear about relationships. Now I just answer, "An average of four hours a day," and move on to the next question, and everyone is happier.

RACISM, BIAS, AND DISCRIMINATION

One of the challenges of committees that are largely or completely lacking diverse members is the potential to be unaware of *systemic racism*, "which refers to the societal disadvantages and inequalities ingrained in a historically racist society over time."[41] Explicit racism is easy to spot and widely regarded as abhorrent in professional settings like search committees. Implicit bias and systemic racism are much harder because they can be difficult to identify. They operate at an unconscious level and can therefore be more insidious. As noted in chapter 5, people with critical thinking skills and empathy are often better at calling it out. The whole committee must be vigilant in recognizing it.

When interviewing candidates, committees should remember the non-neutral context for many candidates. In considering the challenges that academic candidates of color face at universities, Sensoy and DiAngelo refer to W. E. B. Du Bois's term *double consciousness* to describe the additional concerns and considerations that people of color face in interviewing.[42] "Is the campus in a city or a small town? Will I be safe afterhours there? Will I encounter any other people of color (or otherwise minoritized peoples)? What microaggressions will I face, and how do I stay focused in spite of them? Do I speak openly and honestly about my work on race? Do I talk about how my identity shapes my work? Against this backdrop, well-meaning advice by a committee member to 'just be yourself' does not alleviate the multilayered stress a candidate of color may feel."[43]

In the field of art museums, I have heard boards invoke "quality" and "excellence" as the reasons they don't want to pursue a candidate of color. Usually, this means the candidate did not attend an elite university, did not have the correct pool of mentors and contacts, or did not study a field of art traditionally accepted as the canon. This kind of implicit bias is rooted in the defense that your objections are not due to race, gender, sexual orientation, or other forms of bias, but objective reactions to other factors.

Search committees need to be relentless in their quest to understand all candidates' track records in promoting diversity. They should not settle for general platitudes and simple words of commitment. Watch for candidates who dodge the question by claiming things like, "I grew up in a diverse neighborhood"; "I am married to a person of color"; "I like to travel a lot"; etc. Committee members should ribbon questions testing cultural competence throughout their questions and not relegate the topic to a few simple "diversity questions" at the end of the interview. For example, the committee could ask for a list of mentors and/or authors the candidate follows (looking for the inclusion of a diverse roster of influence). What tactics do you use to lead your board into a deeper understanding of DEI in your organization? What are your strategies for hiring diverse candidates? What strategies do you use to ensure that employees of color feel a sense of belonging in your current workplace?

In writing about university search committees, Sensoy and DiAngelo note that responses to questions about diversity and inclusion are rarely taken seriously or considered as a reason not to hire a candidate who is qualified in other areas.[44] When the lack of DEI proficiency and commitment is not taken seriously, the work of the committee becomes performative as members are merely seeking cover. In a classic double standard, BIPOC candidates are expected to be articulate on DEI, but white candidates are often excused from an inability to discuss it. "In our experience, a candidate's response to a question on diversity has never been the determining factor in the decision. In this way, these questions simply function as cover for the committee and the institution itself, as they are rarely taken seriously."[45]

The interview is also the time for an organization to prove its own cultural competence. I am ashamed that I once invited a finalist candidate, whom I later discovered was Muslim, to lunch during Ramadan. The candidate was incredibly gracious, but my lack of sensitivity must have caused concern about me and our institution. The committee and the person putting together the candidate's schedule of meetings should show awareness and ensure that meetings with stakeholder groups and individuals outside the committee contain diverse constituents—and if they don't, candidates should ask why.

BIAS: TEN COMMON BEHAVIORS TO WATCH OUT FOR

1. Search committees should watch out for *confirmation bias*, or the tendency to seek out people and information that confirms existing beliefs. We often give greater credence to information that confirms our own beliefs. It is another example of a kind of mental shortcut in gathering information. Once a committee member establishes a certain expectation for a candidate, such as "I don't think she has the gravitas for the job," they seek evidence to confirm their assumption, rather than accepting new ideas. In discussing the double bind for *Time* magazine, Tannen writes, "The most difficult aspect of the double bind is that it is invisible; we think we are just reacting to the candidates as

individuals."[46] In interviewing two candidates, a committee member who shifts their criteria for the job so that it favors the white candidate is engaging in a form of unintended bias.[47]

2. Challenge phrases like, "I don't think this person is the right fit." Ian Hany Lopez calls "fit" the dog whistle for how committees signal racial bias without admitting it.[48] A number of scholars have published on the use of "not a good fit" as code for class and race.[49] In her studies, Danowitz Sagaria found that conversations about "fit" were a form of determining "cultural capital, such as language, modes of social interaction, and meaning, [and it] reflects the dominant white ideology and is a basis for excluding candidates."[50]

3. Avoid microaggressions, or everyday insults, indignities, and demeaning messages related to someone's gender, race, sexuality, age, or socioeconomic background. These comments are often delivered by well-intentioned people who are unaware that these questions are demeaning. "Essentially, microaggressions are based on a simple, damaging idea: 'Because you are X, you probably are/are not or like/don't like Y.'"[51] Women and candidates of color are often asked more questions about their families and personal lives. Single women are especially targeted for these questions.

4. Avoid the coded language "nontraditional candidates." I cringe when I hear the boards say they are "open to untraditional candidates." It's a loaded phrase and can mean lots of things, but it is often used as a way of saying diverse applicants, which is simply offensive. Avoid the term altogether and be explicit about the kind of candidates you are hoping to see. If you mean someone without a college degree, or someone outside the academic field, just say it.

5. Committees sometimes view the résumés of women and people of color in ways they don't white male candidates. Once, while scrutinizing résumés of potential trustees for a museum, a trustee who did not work outside the home lit upon the biography of a Native American candidate. The trustee blurted out, "Wait a minute. She doesn't have a job. We can't consider her." Not only did the double standard not occur to her, but none of the other trustees in the room noticed it, either. The fact that "whitening your résumé" is an established practice tells you a lot about the problem.[52]

6. In addition, don't assume that diverse candidates will excel at activities like "community engagement." Community engagement should be the responsibility of any nonprofit leader. All candidates should be questioned equally about their experience in this important activity.

7. "I thought they were great and would be good for a deputy director role . . ." It is shocking how often search committees decide women and candidates of color are better suited to the number-two role in an organization. In these cases, committees have responded strongly to their candidate, but they just cannot quite get past their bias to see them in the leadership role. If a committee member suggests this, and others start nodding, the committee should

pause and check for bias. What, exactly, is holding them back from seeing the candidate as the potential leader?

8. Never assume that women and people of color will necessarily have a harder time "hitting the ground running" than a white man. It sounds silly, but I hear this statement often, and it is grounded in the idea that women and people of color are at a disadvantage. It's simply not true.

9. Also, don't think there just aren't people of color in your field and that there will not be many applicants. This becomes a self-fulfilling prophecy for searches that don't want to work too hard. No search committee in America today should accept a candidate pool that is not fully diverse (age, gender, sexuality, race, ethnicity, class, socioeconomic background, etc.).

10. Finally, using the reason, "I don't think they will be a good fit with the staff" as the reason not to proceed with a candidate is unacceptable. Committees sometimes express concern that someone who does not conform to the profile of the previous leader won't be accepted by the staff. There are many problems with this argument, but when it is used about a woman or person of color, it can be an expression of unintended bias.

NOTES

1. David Gaiter, quoted in Tyler Wilde, "GDC 2013: BioWare's David Gaider Asks, 'How about we just decide how not to repel women?'," *PC Gamer*, March 29, 2013, https://www.pcgamer.com/bioware-david-gaider-sex-in-video-game/.

2. Marianne Bertrand and Sendhil Mullainathan, "Are Emily and Greg More Employable Than Lakisha and Jamal? A Field Experiment on Labor Market Discrimination." *American Economic Review*, 94, 4 (September 2004): 991–1013. DOI: 10.1257/0002828042002561; William A. Darity Jr. and Patrick L. Mason, "Evidence on Discrimination in Employment: Codes of Color, Codes of Gender." *Journal of Economic Perspectives*, 12, 2 (Spring 1998): 63–90; Roland Fryer and Steven Levitt, "The Causes and Consequences of Distinctively Black Names," *Quarterly Journal of Economics*, Vol. 119, No. 3 (August 2004): 767–805; Dina Gerdeman, "Minorities Who 'Whiten' Job Résumés Get More Interviews," Harvard Business School, May 17, 2017, https://hbswk.hbs.edu/item/minorities-who-whiten-job-resumes-get-more-interviews.

3. Gerdeman, "Minorities Who 'Whiten' Job Résumés."

4. Bertrand and Mullianathan, "Are Emily and Greg More Employable?"

5. Kathleen Parker, "What Steinem, Albright, and Clinton Don't Get About Millennial Women," *Washington Post*, February 9, 2016, https://www.washingtonpost.com/opinions/what-steinem-albright-and-clinton-dont-get-about-millennial-women/2016/02/09/7d156d80-cf73-11e5-abc9-ea152f0b9561_story.html.

6. Robin Tolmach Lakoff, *Language and Woman's Place* (New York: Oxford University Press, 1975), 61–62.

7. Deborah Tannen, "The Self-Fulfilling Prophecy of Disliking Hillary Clinton," *Time* magazine, March 15, 2016, https://time.com/4258976/disliking-hillary-clinton/.

8. Deborah Tannen, "The Double Bind," in *Thirty Ways of Looking at Hillary: Reflections by Women Writers*, edited by Susan Morrison (New York: HarperCollins, 2008), 135.

9. Kaywin Feldman, "Unpacking 'Gravitas': A Museum Director Reflects on Gender Inequities in the Museum Field," *Museum*, March–April 2017, https://www.aam-us.org/wp-content/uploads/2017/10/unpacking-gravitas-1-1.pdf.

10. Gerry Valentine, "Executive Presence: What Is It, Why You Need It and How to Get It," *Forbes*, July 31, 2018, https://www.forbes.com/sites/forbescoachescouncil/2018/07/31/executive-presence-what-is-it-why-you-need-it-and-how-to-get-it/?sh=5224ff246bc7.

11. Valentine, "Executive Presence."

12. Sylvia Ann Hewlett, "The New Rules of Executive Presence," *Harvard Business Review*, January–February 2024, https://hbr.org/2024/01/the-new-rules-of-executive-presence.

13. Inga Bielińska, "Executive Presence Is Being Reframed in the Modern World," *Forbes*, February 6, 2023, https://www.forbes.com/sites/forbescoachescouncil/2023/02/06/executive-presence-is-being-reframed-in-the-modern-world/?sh=6bc947ee51d5.

14. "The Data on Women Leaders," Pew Research Center, September 27, 2023, https://www.pewresearch.org/social-trends/fact-sheet/the-data-on-women-leaders/.

15. Heather Murphy, "Picture a Leader. Is She a Woman?" *New York Times*, March 16, 2018, https://www.nytimes.com/2018/03/16/health/women-leadership-workplace.html.

16. Veronica Treviño, Zannie Giraud Voss, Christine Anagnos, and Alison D. Wade, "The Ongoing Gender Gap in Art Museum Directorships," March 22, 2017, https://aamd.org/sites/default/files/document/AAMD%20NCAR%20Gender%20Gap%202017.pdf.

17. Treviño, Voss, Anagnos, and Wade, "The Ongoing Gender Gap."

18. Kate Zernike, "The Campus Wars Aren't About Gender . . . Are They?" *New York Times*, January 28, 2024, https://www.nytimes.com/2024/01/28/us/colleges-antisemitism-gender.html.

19. Peter Beinart, "Fear of a Female President," *Atlantic*, October 2016, https://www.theatlantic.com/magazine/archive/2016/10/fear-of-a-female-president/497564/.

20. Alice Eagly and Linda L. Carli, "Women and the Labyrinth of Leadership," *Harvard Business Review*, September 2007, https://hbr.org/2007/09/women-and-the-labyrinth-of-leadership.

21. Eagly and Carli, "Women and the Labyrinth of Leadership."

22. Chamorro-Premuzic and Gallop, "7 Leadership Lessons Men Can Learn from Women."

23. Katherine Lanpher, "The Conversation: Donna Brazille and Deborah Tannen Discuss Our Hillary Problem," *More*, October 2007.

24. Eagly and Carli, "Women and the Labyrinth of Leadership"; Wei Zheng, Ronit Kark and Alyson Meister, "How Women Manage the Gendered Norms of Leadership," *Harvard Business Review*, November 28, 2018, https://hbr.org/2018/11/how-women-manage-the-gendered-norms-of-leadership; Tomas Chamorro-Premuzic,

"If Women Are Better Leaders, Then Why Are They Not in Charge?" *Forbes*, May 7, 2021, https://www.forbes.com/sites/tomaspremuzic/2021/03/07/if-women-are-better-leaders-then-why-are-they-not-in-charge/?sh=4116ae756c88.

25. Shari Kendall and Deborah Tannen, "Gender and Language in the Workplace," in Gender and Discourse, ed. Ruth Wodak (New York: Sage Publications, Inc., 1997), 81. https://psycnet.apa.org/doi/10.4135/9781446250204.n5.
26. Joseph C. Rost, *Leadership for the 21st Century* (New York: Praeger, 1991), 102.
27. Eagly and Carli, "Women and the Labyrinth of Leadership"; Chamorro-Premuzic, "If Women Are Better Leaders."
28. Anna Fels, *Necessary Dreams: Ambition in Women's Changing Lives* (New York: Anchor Books, 2004), 50.
29. Anna Fels, "Do Women Lack Ambition?" *Harvard Business Review*, April 2004, https://hbr.org/2004/04/do-women-lack-ambition.
30. Amanda Taub, "Why Are Women-Led Nations Doing Better with Covid-19?" *New York Times*, May 15, 2020, https://www.nytimes.com/2020/05/15/world/coronavirus-women-leaders.html.
31. Stefanie K. Johnson, "2021 Is a Tipping Point for Female Leaders," *Bloomberg*, January 31, 2021, https://www.bloomberg.com/opinion/articles/2021-01-31/women-leaders-are-doing-better-during-the-pandemic#xj4y7vzkg; Michal Katz, "The COVID Crisis Shows Why We Need More Female Leadership," *Fortune*, March 17, 2021, https://fortune.com/2021/03/17/covid-female-women-leadership-jacinda-ardern/; June B. Luscombe, "Jacinda Ardern Helped New Zealand Beat Cornavirus. Next Up: Getting Re-elected," *Time*, June 12, 2020, https://time.com/5852567/new-zealand-coronavirus-jacinda-ardern-election/.
32. Supriya Garikipati and Uma Kambhampati, "Leading the Fight Against the Pandemic: Does Gender 'Really' Matter?" *Feminist Economics*, 27:1–2 (June 3, 2020), 401–18, https://doi.org/10.1080/13545701.2021.1874614.
33. Garikipati and Kambhampati, "Leading the Fight Against the Pandemic."
34. Garikipati and Kambhampati, "Leading the Fight Against the Pandemic."
35. Deborah Tannen, "The Power of Talk: Who Gets Heard and Why," *Harvard Business Review*, September–October 1995, https://hbr.org/1995/09/the-power-of-talk-who-gets-heard-and-why.
36. Tannen, "The Power of Talk."
37. Deborah Tannen, *You Just Don't Understand: Women and Men in Conversation* (New York: Ballantine Books, 1990), 49–50.
38. Tannen, *You Just Don't Understand*, 49–50.
39. Deborah Tannen, *You're the Only One I Can Tell* (New York: Ballantine Books, 2017), 27.
40. Tannen, *You Just Don't Understand*, 49–61.
41. Porter Braswell, "This is the Difference Between Racism and Racial Bias," *Fast Company*, October 19, 2022, https://www.fastcompany.com/90796690/this-is-the-difference-between-racism-and-racial-bias.
42. Sensoy and DiAngelo, "'We Are All for Diversity, but . . .'"
43. Sensoy and DiAngelo, "'We Are All for Diversity, but . . .'"
44. Sensoy and DiAngela, "'We Are All for Diversity, but . . .'"
45. Sensoy and DiAngela, "'We Are All for Diversity, but . . .'"
46. Tannen, "The Self-Fulfilling Prophecy of Disliking Hillary Clinton."

47. John Dovidio, "Understanding Your Racial Biases, with John Dovidio, PhD," in *Speaking of Psychology*, produced by the American Psychological Association, https://www.apa.org/news/podcasts/speaking-of-psychology/understanding-biases.

48. Ian Hany López, *Dog Whistle Politics: How Coded Racial Appeals Have Reinvented Racism and Wrecked the Middle Class* (Oxford, UK: Oxford University Press, 2015), 27.

49. Sensoy and DiAngelo, "'We Are All for Diversity, but . . .'"; Roman Liera and Cheryl Ching, "Reconceptualizing 'Merit' and 'Fit': An Equity-Minded Approach to Hiring," in *Higher Education Administration for Social Justice and Equity*, ed. A. Kezar and J. Posselt (New York: Routledge, 2019), 111–31; Franklin A. Tuitt, Mary Ann Danowitz Sagaria, and Caroline Sotello Viernes Turner, "Signals and Strategies in Hiring Faculty of Color," in *Higher Education: Handbook of Theory and Research,* ed. John C. Smart, Vol. 22, (2007), 497–535; *Debunking the Myth of Job Fit in Higher Education and Student Affairs,* ed. Brian J. Reece, Vu T. Tran, Elliott N. DeVore, and Gabby Porcaro (New York: Stylus Publishing, 2019).

50. Mary Ann Danowitz Sagaria, "An Exploratory Model of Filtering in Administrative Searches: Toward Counter-Hegemonic Discourses," *Journal of Higher Education,* 73, no. 6 (2002): 677–710, http://www.jstor.org/stable/1558402.

51. Ella Washington, "Recognizing and Responding to Microaggressions at Work," *Harvard Business Review*, May 10, 2022, https://hbr.org/2022/05/recognizing-and-responding-to-microaggressions-at-work.

52. Ellen Brait, "'Résumé Whitening' Doubles Callbacks for Minority Job Candidates, Study Finds," *Guardian*, March 17, 2016, https://www.theguardian.com/world/2016/mar/17/jobs-search-hiring-racial-discrimination-resume-whitening-callbacks; Michael Luo, "'Whitening' the Résumé," *New York Times*, December 5, 2009, https://www.nytimes.com/2009/12/06/weekinreview/06Luo.html; Bourree Lam, "When Résumés Are Made 'White' to Please Potential Employers," *Atlantic*, March 23, 2016, https://www.theatlantic.com/business/archive/2016/03/white-resume-diversity/475032/.

7

The First Six Months

Congratulations, you got the job; now you have to earn it. —Lloyd Braun, former CEO of ABC Entertainment[1]

GETTING STARTED

While the one-hundred-day mark is arbitrary, it is important to begin a new CEO tenure understanding that your first year will be extremely busy and filled with pressure, deadlines, high expectations, and stress. I find it helpful to think of three onboarding phases: prior to arrival; the first six months; the next six to fourteen months. For both first-time CEOs and experienced CEOs, the first year is overwhelmingly challenging.

A new move requires a mindset shift. Whether your prior role was as CEO or senior executive, you were probably highly competent and successful. You knew the players, the community, the risks, and the pitfalls, and you had a strategy and support from your stakeholders. On day one at your new job, you have none of that, even if you were an internal candidate. The mindset shift required is to realize that the new you *is* different from the old you because the context has changed. It's disorienting and can feel like you are going back to "square one"—and you are. As you approach your new role, do so with a growth mindset, knowing that your primary job for your first year is to learn and to do so quickly and with humility and curiosity.

> As people learn new skills, they go from unconsciously incompetent (don't know what they don't know) to consciously incompetent (know what they don't know and aren't happy about it) to consciously competent (can do with deliberative thinking) to unconsciously competent (can do intuitively). When you move into a new organization or a meaningfully different new role, you go from being competent to incompetent. If you're unconsciously incompetent you're going to get into trouble because you'll be relying on your old intuitions.

If you're consciously incompetent you can ratchet yourself up to conscious competence with deliberative thinking. . . . Knowing that, you can consciously resist the allure of your intuition, ignore your initial impressions and push yourself to take the more deliberate, controlled, effortful, rule-governed way of thinking through things required to increase your chances of success. — George Bradt, 2017[2]

WHY THE FIRST ONE-HUNDRED-DAY OBSESSION?

We have President Franklin Delano Roosevelt to thank for the institutionalized focus on a first one-hundred-day plan. When FDR was inaugurated on March 4, 1933, he committed to an aggressive plan to aid a nation suffering the worst effects of the Great Depression. Congress was not scheduled to be in session, but Roosevelt summoned them to Washington and working together, they passed a series of important bills and laws. On the one-hundredth day of his presidency, FDR addressed the nation and reported on the progress made over his first three months in office, forever cementing the importance of a one-hundred-day plan.[3]

Roosevelt determined that rescuing banks was the most critical first step to help Americans, and the Emergency Banking Act was passed within 5 days of his inauguration. Working with Congress, he then rolled out a number of acts focused on fixing the economic problems that were crippling the nation and causing widespread suffering. His plan was to aid distressed families; expand public works; rescue farms and farming; prop up securities and investments; and support the creation of jobs and relief. One of his most popular initiatives, the repeal of Prohibition, also occurred in his first one hundred days.[4]

An ambitous leader's first initiatives cannot all be successful, which Roosevelt acknowledged. Speaking at Oglethorpe University in the run-up to the 1932 presidential election, he said, "The country needs and . . . the country demands bold, persistent experimentation. It is common sense to take a method and try it. If it fails, admit it frankly and try another. But above all, try something."[5]

The nonprofit CEO starting a new tenure can learn from Roosevelt's approach with the following lessons:

- Arrive with optimism tempered by some realistic truth-telling.
- Describe a plan and establish achievable wins during a specified period.
- Identify and prioritize the most transformative initial win to enable the progress that follows.
- Follow up with additional goals as the work evolves.
- Maintain regular communication (through "fireside chats") that keep people updated on progress.
- Communicate a timeline that people can follow.

- Remember that rituals matter.
- Celebrate the milestones and lay the groundwork for the next set of goals.

PRIOR TO ARRIVAL

As soon as a candidate accepts a new CEO role, their life is upended. Emotions run high not only for the new CEO and their family, but also for the staff, board, and institutional stakeholders at the old institution and the new one. Guilt, fear of failure, anticipation of the unknown, and the complexities of a move can be overwhelming. Carl Bass, when asked to take over as CEO of Autodesk, said, "I hid in the bathroom for five days. . . . I thought, this is not for me. I don't want to do it. I don't have the skills to do it."[6] In his survey of life transitions, Bruce Feiler observes that fear is the most common emotion that people experience during a life transition. He notes that fear can also be good; it motivates and pushes us to expand our horizons and reach new heights.[7]

On numerous occasions in my life, when confronted with embarking on something new, with significant life consequences, I have experienced this kind of fear. It's a special kind of fear because it is self-induced, not a result of something happening to me. This fear is initiated by something inside that pushes me to challenge myself, to choose risk over regret for roads not taken. It appears to me that in our post-COVID-19 world, people are now somewhat more likely to shy away from the personal challenge decisions that invoke fear. In a spate of recent failed searches, I have watched finalists for terrific senior positions offering great career advancement decline offers at the very last minute. They all cite the fear of upheaval, the fear of leaving a comfortable and known life, and the fear of trying something big and new as the reasons for not making the change. I have experienced that fear many times, so I understand it. As Feiler writes, "Fear is innate. Fearlessness can be learned."[8]

I recommend that everyone go into a major life transition expecting an emotional roller coaster and preparing for it. An intense new job takes a toll on our emotional and physical health. Be kind to yourself—and to your family members, who are along on the ride. This period is difficult for family members who are managing their own apprehensiveness, especially if it involves a move and the strain of the logistics of a move. Give yourself the time and mental space to resolve relocation details, and don't let it compound the stress of your transition. To make it all harder, your family will see much less of you as you will be absorbed by the onboarding of your new role and extraordinary demands on your time. No wonder it is often advised that family members trail the arrival of a new CEO by several months if a move is involved. In all my moves, my husband and cats have arrived several months after I started in my new role, and it was helpful for all of us due to the long hours, arrival stress, and complications of the move. On second thought, the cats didn't really care.

PREPARING FOR THE NEW ROLE

"It was like I was going away to war" is how one business leader described the process of preparing for a new leadership role.[9] There are a number of valuable books about the first one hundred days, and they generally agree that a leader who succeeds at leadership onboarding will be set up for a successful tenure in their new role.[10] Someone who wastes this period and stumbles will have a much harder time succeeding in the role. It is not impossible to recover, but it will be much more difficult. One-third to one-half of corporate CEOs fail in their first twelve to eighteen months.[11] Remember, the greatest number of airline accidents happen at takeoff and landing. The initial arrival period is so critical to your future success that you must be thoughtful and strategic in your planning for it.

After the exhilaration of the announcement passes, it is time to buckle down and prepare for the new role. Bradt, Check, and Pedraza refer to this period as "the fuzzy front end" and note that the job starts the day you accept the offer.[12] Assuming that a leader gives a couple months' notice to their current employer, they should not waste this time. It is tempting to focus one's attention on wrapping up current work and trying to delay the impact of the transition. It is also common to double down on control at the current institution due to departure guilt and frustrated feelings of being seen as a lame duck. Your transition, however, begins the day after the public announcement, and you need to invest your time and emotional energy in your future.

In their survey of over sixty corporate leaders, Dan Ciampa and Michael Watkins note that most of the leaders "admitted wishing, once they were on board and some time had gone by, that they had been better prepared prior to joining."[13] A search consultant once gave me the advice that while you should not abandon your current institution, your loyalty needs to transition to your new institution at this point. It may feel like you are betraying your institution after years of dedication and hard work given for a place and people that you have come to care about deeply. Your successful landing in your new role, however, dictates that you need to prioritize this next organization now.

During this interim period, use your time to learn, plan, listen, and invest in future relationships. Working with trustees and senior leaders at your new institution, try to get access to as many background reading materials as possible. Take everything you can get your hands on. There is usually a wealth of detailed proprietary information that organizations do not send to candidates, so now is your chance. Items you should seek include the last three or four annual audits and recent financial statements; bylaws; board orientation materials; staff meeting agendas; new employee handbook; publications; articles, books, and essays about the history of the institution; policy documents; strategic plans; organizational charts with senior leader biographies; white papers;

recent media coverage; and social media posts of key staff and stakeholders—to name only a few sources.

Before your arrival, it is good to establish contact with key trustees, staff, and patrons. Ideally, you will discover a few senior members of the staff whom you trust and who can advise you on the right people to meet with in your first week. Before arriving at one institution, I was contacted directly by several staff members, who asked to meet with me my first week. I did not have the sense to seek advice first and later discovered that I'd met with the wrong people (the people with a singular self-serving agenda—and everyone else but me knew it). Not only was it a poor use of my time, but watchful staff members were concerned that I was investing valuable time in the wrong place.

If possible, connect with civic leaders and community stakeholders who can give you perspective on the community, the institution, and this moment in its history. You have a short period without baggage to do fact-finding and interviews. This process will continue after you have arrived, but it is good to access as much information and background as possible before you begin. You should also exploit your network. Seek advice from mentors, colleagues, and advisors.

TIME FOR SELF-REFLECTION

> We spend a lot of time teaching leaders what to stop. Half the leaders I have met don't need to learn what to do. They need to learn what to stop. —Peter Drucker[14]

This period is also an important time of self-reflection. One of the hardest lessons I learned in my last transition was that I could not compare my leadership at the end of my eleven-year tenure in Minneapolis with that of my first few months at the National Gallery. While the job is similar, the people, the context, the challenges, the scale, and the opportunities have all changed. In starting a new role, you are beginning a new era for your leadership and personal development. Use the time between jobs to think about your skill set and opportunities for growth, trying to anticipate the new challenges you will confront.

One of the books that I send to people making a job transition is Marshall Goldsmith's excellent *What Got You Here Won't Get You There*. Goldsmith, an executive coach, argues that many of the qualities that help to successfully propel people to leadership roles hold them back from advancing further, which he calls "the paradox of success."[15] Goldsmith's experience has shown him that successful executives become blinkered by their success, as a form of cognitive dissonance. We believe that something is true, and we filter all information, even contradictory information, through that lens. Goldsmith argues that in coaching leaders, he cannot fix problems of skill, personality, or intelligence. He writes that it is interpersonal and leadership behavioral flaws that successful leaders need to be aware of as their careers advance.[16]

During this time, lay out your plans for how you will approach your first three months. Work with the chair of the board and any other key trustees to ensure that you understand their expectations and that you have a mutually agreed-upon process. A big mistake that some new leaders make is to passively allow the new institution to create their schedule and make plans for them. You often don't know whom to listen to, and before you know it, your calendar is full, without regard to the most strategic way for you to use your time. Having listened to the advice of trusted advisors, you must be in control of your agenda, communicating priorities and how you want to use your time most effectively.

If possible, it is helpful to have a "soft start," in which you arrive before your official start day. I have never been able to do this because I feel squeezed between the old institution wanting me to stay as long as possible and the new one wanting me to start as soon as possible. If you can manage to do so, however, it is the best kind of onboarding. This unannounced first day or week enables you to expand the time that you have to learn and absorb your new institution before the true first-day pressure begins.

Whenever it is, plan your first day. Think about what you wear, which offices you visit, what you do for lunch, whom you meet with and for how long. What you say to people in the halls will be watched, discussed, and combed for messages and signals. Think through every single aspect of the day and be prepared for your first internal messages. What are the signals that you want to send early on? How will you arrive? How will you tell your new team about yourself?

You will want to address the staff in person on your first day. I find it difficult to stand in front of a new staff, speaking at length about myself—but that's what they want to hear. They don't really want to hear about your degrees and accomplishments, and they certainly don't want to hear about your former employer and how terrific everything was. They want to understand what kind of person you are and what motivates you. Your first presentation is your opportunity to talk about what has made you the person you are, to share what you value, and to tell the staff about your family. People respond to great storytellers, so remember that you are telling your story. Whatever you do, don't use a PowerPoint deck. People don't want a business presentation; they want to get to know *you*.

They will also want to hear that you are excited about this new role, ready to work hard, and grateful for their work in getting the organization to its current position. Staff will want to know that you are excited to be a part of the community and that you value a sense of place and your organization's role in the life of the community. Avoid descriptions of your plans and ideas for the organization at this early stage and keep the moment focused on the team getting to know you as a person. Be gracious, acknowledge your predecessor and the board, and credit the staff of the place you are leaving for the institution's success and the reputation of the staff of your new organization as one of the reasons that you took the job.

A compelling personal vision is tied to the leader's credibility. In a world without enough principled leaders with vision, we sure talk about vision a lot. A credible leader needs to be someone who can articulate a passionate personal vision for the work. This vision is related to, but different from, an organization's mission and vision. It is a summation of a leader's professional purpose, and in mission-based organizations like nonprofits, it likely overlaps with the mission of the organization. It is formed by the CEO's life experiences, their values, and their belief that the nonprofit will make a difference in the world. Your vision will tell audiences who you are, what you stand for, and what excites you.

In articulating your personal vision, it is helpful to start with a story that offers insight into who you are and what brings value to your life. You want to use your vision to describe an optimistic and impactful future for the organization, using concrete descriptions that help people to see that future.

In my work as the director of an art museum, my personal vision revolves around my belief that art enhances, and sometimes changes, lives. Museums enable us to come together in social settings and experience triumphs of human creativity, across time and across global cultures. In doing so, we often experience awe, empathy, and curiosity, all of which help us to experience our shared humanity. We become less narcissistic, less pessimistic, and more open to hope, love, inclusion, and the beauty of the lived human experience. I have devoted my life's work to this vision, and as times become more complicated and despairing, I am more convinced than ever of the importance of this mission, and I express it almost daily.

THE FIRST ONE HUNDRED DAYS: BE SURE TO PAINT THE LOBBY

> If you can't get some things moving in six months, you're a dead duck.—
> Ciampa and Watkins, *Right from the Start* [17]

When I started in Memphis, a hospital CEO on the board told me that I needed to "paint the lobby." He explained that hospital administrators know that soon after their arrival, they need to paint the lobby, so that everyone would know the new leader was doing something. He meant his advice metaphorically, and I have never forgotten the important role of "painting the lobby" shortly after arrival. Doing something immediately that is highly visible but not terribly disruptive signals to staff and stakeholders that there is a new CEO who is eager, decisive, and ready to make necessary changes. Although it is human nature to be apprehensive about change, few people are energized by the thought of working for a passive caretaker without a vision.

When I arrived at the National Gallery, I discovered that the museum did not host regular all-staff meetings or send out regular staff communications. So, I "painted the lobby" by starting a new internal communications program in my first week. McKinsey has noted that in the corporate world, "CEOs who make these moves [resource allocation, programmatic changes, industry differentiation] earlier in their tenure outperform those who move later, and those who do so multiple times in their tenure avoid an otherwise common decline in performance."[18]

Create a Map of Your Stakeholders

Whom do you need to meet in your first thirty, sixty, and ninety days? This will require juggling staff, trustees, donors, media, peers, community leaders, and elected officials. Even in a small organization, you can't possibly meet them all in ninety days, so be strategic about how you use your time. Prioritize the people who will help you to be successful in this early period, and be sure you are keeping your commitment to diversity and inclusion top of mind as you develop your key stakeholder lists. As your time in the role increases, your opportunities for connections will also expand. In these early meetings, read people carefully (noting both verbal and nonverbal cues) as you want to find the people who could become trusted advisors. It's very difficult in the early days to ascertain who might become your confidants. The challenge here is that trust takes time to build, and in this early stage, you don't have much of that. Rely on your instincts and insightful reading of people and their motivations. Watch out for factions and partisan agendas and people you may be alienating inadvertently by the advisors you pick—and those you don't pick. Remain highly attuned to office politics.

> When you become a leader, it is as if you are on a stage with a microphone at all times. It's a hot mike 24-7. —Mary Elizabeth Porray[19]

In addition to figuring out whom you should trust, you need to be focused on earning stakeholder trust and confidence. This is done by telling and showing—telling people about yourself and your values and then using those values to make decisions and communicating with authenticity. People are watching you with binoculars, analyzing your every move and trying to anticipate where you will likely go next. They are reading you out of self-interest, trying to figure out if you will be beneficial to their career advancement and agenda. Watch out for the small, offhand comments that are interpreted (or manipulated) as directives. I joke that if I say I like spring because the grass is so green, I will hear someone say, "The new director wants everything to be colored green."

People are watching you closely as they try to figure out what kind of person you are; they want to know if you are consistent and authentic. Showing up with vulnerability helps. As noted in chapter 6, society has taught us that leaders are competent and confident figures with authority. Authors such as Hubert Joly and Brené Brown argue that courageous leaders show vulnerability.[20] Research by Paula Niedenthal, professor of psychology at the University of Wisconsin-Madison, reveals that people are naturally able to read inauthenticity.[21] We are often able to see through people who are inauthentic, and therefore we are unable to connect with them. Yale School of Management professor Emma Seppala points out that we feel more comfortable and trusting around people whom we perceive to be vulnerable and authentic.[22] Employees with authentic leaders tend to be happier at work, be more trustful, and stay longer, ultimately leading to higher performance. So, in those early days of town halls and meetings, show up as your authentic self and don't be afraid to project vulnerability.

Take a Listening Tour

Your first three months should be used for intense listening. If you have read and absorbed as much background information prior to arrival, your job now is to listen and internalize what you hear. Leaders tend to be better talkers than they are listeners, so this is probably a good time to sharpen your listening skills. In her engaging book *You're Not Listening*, *New York Times* reporter Kate Murphy points out how to not just passively hear people talking, but to actively listen.[23] Murphy describes "shift response," where we listen only long enough to shift the conversation away from the speaker and to ourselves.[24] She also emphasizes the importance of asking drill-down questions, especially looking for ways to understand how the speaker feels emotionally about what they are telling you. Murphy recommends that a listener should be a detective, asking, "Why is this person telling me this?"[25] If someone says they are disappointed in a colleague, ask them why. Ask them how the colleague might have handled the situation differently. Ask them how the colleague's behavior made them feel and how they responded at the time. By asking more questions, we reach a greater understanding of the motivations of the employee and the situation at hand—and that is the job of a leader. In listening, pay close attention to the specific words used. You can hear metamessages and nuance if you are attuned to the specific words a person decides to use. As noted in chapter 5, keep in mind Deborah Tannen's comments about how men and women tend to communicate differently so that you can read between the lines of communication styles and detect metamessages.

Some people are born as better listeners than others, but we can all hone our skills with some conscious commitment to the practice. Guy Itzchakov suggests that active listening includes three key features: paying very close attention, demonstrated by maintaining direct eye contact; comprehension, which is confirmed by paraphrasing what you have heard; and positive intention, or being nonjudgmental about what you hear. He notes that "listening is like a muscle that needs training."[26]

Active listening also involves the nonverbal clues that people give us all the time—facial expressions, intonation, body language, and mannerisms. Murphy notes that "at least 55% of the emotional content of a spoken message is, in fact, transmitted nonverbally."[27] Having been raised by a volatile parent, from a young age I developed an acute ability to read nonverbal messages. I often sense the actions of employees, such as the decision to resign, before they verbally announce a decision. A leadership coach once described it as having giant insect antennae on the top of my head, enabling me to sense and read nonverbal cues.

Even though all the advance research and reading work is critical, it does not replace the need to spend your first four to six months listening. It is from meeting people and actively listening that you understand the "people part" of the business, such as values, behavioral expectations, institutional culture, and internal politics and factions. Few of these parts of an organization are obvious to outsiders (often, even trustees don't know much of this part of the business). Active listening also shows the staff that you are the sort of leader who values them and their expertise. Who doesn't just want to be heard?

In my first five months at the National Gallery, I met with nearly every staff member (one thousand people) in seventy meetings of departmental groups of between five and twelve people. "As the new leader, you're generally given the benefit of the doubt. I think it's your one chance to ask stupid questions," says Robert Eckert, chief executive of Mattel.[28] During my listening sessions, I talked very little, and I never talked about myself, but instead I asked all the questions. After learning names, roles, and tenures of all the people in the room, I asked each group the same questions:

- You are talented and could work anywhere. Why do you work *here*? What do you love about it?
- What annoys you? What could we do better; what should change?
- What is so core to who we are that it should never change?
- How do you think the public perceives us? Why?
- What advice do you have for me?

Throughout each meeting, I took notes. I didn't delegate this function as I wanted to be sure I was recording what I heard, and not through someone else's interpretation of what they heard and observed. I promised that no comment would be attributed and that I would review my notes, ensuring that their generosity in sharing their time and opinions with me would not be wasted. Five years later, I occasionally reference these notes and share certain aspects with new senior leaders as part of their onboarding, so I am still reaping rewards of the time invested.

In reporting back at an all-staff meeting after my listening sessions, I used my notes to create word clouds, showing the common themes across the institution. I then boiled down what I heard over the listening sessions into six primary themes. When presenting back what you hear, offer a positive picture of future opportunity. Nobody wants to hear a presentation from the new CEO about what's broken in the institution and needs to change. Instead, present a hopeful and optimistic vision of the future that everyone wants to see. "It's easier to follow someone with all of your heart if you know where you are headed, if the path chosen makes sense, and if the role you can play on the journey is clear."[29] After describing what success would look like in each of the six focus areas, I listed around six possible specific first steps. A recent review of the forty initiatives listed revealed that we have completed over 90 percent of them.

In addition to formal meetings like the ones described above, I am a big believer in informal small coffees and lunches with individuals and small groups. The purpose of these informal meetings is to show interest in the people who work at the organization. In all the places that I have worked, these more informal interactions have enabled people to speak more openly about their motivations and emotions. People are eager to tell their stories and are generally grateful that someone—especially the boss—takes the time to hear them and recognize their point of view.

THE PLAN

> What *should* my contribution be? To answer it, they must address three distinct elements: What does the situation require? Given my strengths, my way of performing, and my values, how can I make the greatest contribution to what needs to be done? And finally, what results have to be achieved to make a difference? —Peter Drucker[30]

Somewhere around the first five or six months, you want to present an initial plan and build momentum. This early in your tenure, it will be the first phase of a plan that will take multiple steps to complete. In these early days, you don't want to look too far ahead because the landscape and the opportunities will change after you have been in the role for a few years. You want some bold projects that require a stretch—but are not impossible to achieve. Your plan needs to be written and should be concrete, including specific action steps, accountability, and a timeline.

I have always found it hard to prioritize at this point as my instinct is to want to fix or change everything at once. Resist this urge, as it is critical that you prioritize the work and not get distracted by biting off too much. You need the time to understand the organization's capacity and the strengths, weaknesses, and abilities of your team members. By not focusing, you run the risk of wearing people out, confusing them about priorities, and jeopardizing your ability to deliver on quick wins. You want to build coalitions of support for the change you want to see.

Usually, but not always, you will know before starting in your new role whether the institution is in crisis (financial, reputational, programmatic, governance, etc.). I always like to think of operations as a car engine, and you should know if the warning light is illuminated on some part of the dashboard. If the warning light is on, this is clearly where you need to focus your early work. In two of the museums I have led, I inherited significant structural deficits when I arrived, and resolving a financial crisis clearly needed to be the initial focus of our work.

When Hubert Joly took over Best Buy in 2012, most people expected the business to fail, much like its competitor, Circuit City. The month after Joly started, the cover of *Bloomberg Businessweek* showed a zombie wearing a Best Buy uniform. Joly realized that "during a turnaround, the priority is to create the energy needed to save a dying business. It means coming up with a good plan fast; focusing everyone on clear, simple priorities; and making the environment intense but safe."[31] The Best Buy board gave Joly fifty-seven days to come up with a plan, so Joly had to disregard his McKinsey discipline in creating long-term complex plans.

Joly surmised that the company had two problems: revenues were down, and margins were down. Instead of trying to fix everything at once, he focused the team on growing revenues and growing margins.[32] Just a few months after Best Buy launched their new plan, nicknamed "Renew Blue," they announced that sales were flat—and celebrated. This result was far better than the bankruptcy everyone predicted, and the company felt wind at its back.

The story of the turnaround at Best Buy has lots of lessons for a new leader, including the process of creating a quick and focused short-term plan when the dashboard warning light is on and needs urgent attention. It is also the story of an experienced CEO overcoming fear and taking the leap into an industry in which he had little experience, during a crisis. Joly approached the role with humility, authenticity, vulnerability, and an optimistic belief in humanity (which he refers to as "human magic"). Joly arrived at Best Buy as a talented and experienced leader, and in the process of transforming the company, he also transformed into an even better and more effective leader.

As much as possible, your plan should reflect information shared during listening sessions and your internalized understanding of the organization's mission and history. In this process, you will have learned about the organization's audience/constituents; the institutional culture and talent; potential partners; and conditions for success. Establish some frameworks for measuring progress so that people know how they will know when they have been successful. Wherever possible in your verbal and written presentations, use quotes from the founder and/or other influential figures in the institution's history. To this day, I frequently comment on the profundity of the National Gallery's dedication on the eve of the United States' entry into the Second World War.

At the time of our dedication on March 17, 1941, President Franklin Delano Roosevelt said, "The dedication of this Gallery to a living past, and to a greater and more richly living future, is the measure of the earnestness of our intention: that the freedom of the human spirit shall go on."[33]

Shortly after his arrival, I had the pleasure of hearing Joseph Haj, artistic director of the Guthrie Theater in Minneapolis, talk about his vision for the Guthrie. Someone in the audience commented sympathetically that times were difficult for the arts. Haj asserted that these were not hard times, but perhaps a golden age. He asked the audience to think of Tyrone Guthrie, putting a shovel in the frozen winter ground of Minneapolis to build a theater out of nothing. Seven years later, I remember his comments because Joe didn't take the pity opportunity offered to him, but instead he used the founding of the theater to remind his audience that great things come from sacrifice and struggle and to align people around his optimistic sense of purpose.

THE ROLE OF THE BOARD IN THE FIRST SIX MONTHS

Boards often miss just how complicated and difficult CEO transitions are and confuse leadership transitions with onboarding. Boards can underestimate the work that a new CEO needs to do to build coalitions and navigate internal politics. They set business expectations for business results, but not necessarily the harder ones around culture and power dynamics.[34]

Trustees quite rightly understand that one of their important responsibilities is to introduce a new CEO to the community. The trustees who are most socially active embrace this opportunity with verve, but the entire board should help in this arena. People with influence in the community have huge weight, and who introduces the new CEO can make a difference. In addition to hosting lunches and parties, trustees need to be talking up the new CEO as they are out and about in the community. It is their job to sell the CEO and their vision to their peers. While it is natural for some trustees to do this, it helps when board leadership stresses that this is everyone's job and holds them accountable to do it.

Trusted advisors and important trustees will be the first audience for the CEO's initial plan. To be successful, a new leader needs an inspirational vision, a bold plan, and a supportive board. CEOs and boards often enjoy their best relationship during the first few years of the CEO's tenure because trustees feel they are needed and that they have a stake in their leader's success. They are excited about the new opportunities for the organization and for their potential role in helping to implement the new vision. Board leadership should repeatedly remind trustees that their most important responsibility after the CEO has been hired is to ensure their success.

Socializing the plan with the board can be a challenge, especially with large boards. If the plan has staff changes and disruptions, confidentiality becomes difficult—I have never seen a board that doesn't include several people who enjoy a good gossip at cocktail parties. This is the time for board leadership to rise to the challenge. They will want to hear the thoughts, ideas, and concerns of their board, but their most important job is to ensure support for the CEO. The executive committee, functioning as a kind of kitchen cabinet, should actively debate and advise behind closed doors. But when the doors open, they must be unanimously aligned with the CEO and around the organization's mission.

The CEO and board chair will work out the cadence of their new relationship. Across four institutions, I have worked with fifteen different board chairs, and I have chaired two boards. Each of my board relationships was different, and I learned early on that it is my responsibility to adapt to the chair's style and their needs from me. They have ranged from wanting a regular meeting schedule in person to ad-hoc telephone check-ins. Finding the right rhythm of the relationship can be difficult for the first few months after a new appointment.

A new CEO sometimes must ease a chair out of hands-on management, as they often become accustomed to an increased management role and physical presence during the period of leadership transition. On one occasion, shortly after I arrived, I had to ask a board chair to stop attending all staff meetings as it made it appear that he didn't trust me. He was attending because he had grown to enjoy them, and he was disappointed to step away but understood the request. While it is your job to adapt to your chair, you may still need to set some boundaries. Becoming accustomed to this new relationship can be challenging when you are new to an organization, and you are unproven and therefore more vulnerable.

As the blush of the honeymoon phase wears off, any leader who is doing their job is certain to disappoint or aggravate some institutional stakeholders who do not agree with new directions or priorities. This usually occurs when a trustee, patron, or staff member fears losing something they care deeply about: an audience, a program, an event, or a fundraising initiative. They sense the institution's shifting of priorities, and this makes them, and their priorities, feel less important or relevant. Of course, leadership wants to minimize the times this happens and the negative impact that change can effect, but it is an inevitable occurrence of effective new leadership. Trustees need to be ready to stand up for their new CEO in these circumstances.

THE PREDECESSOR

I have long thought that industry membership organizations should hold a session on how to be a gracious predecessor. I have seen and experienced some poor behavior from former CEOs toward their successors. It can sometimes be challenging, but new CEOs should have empathy for the person whom they succeed. Nonprofit careers are rarely merely a professional calling, and most of us have our own passions, values, and identities rolled into our work. It is painful to pass the baton to someone else and witness changes to the organization you helped to steward.

And of course, the number-one rule is to never, ever be publicly critical of your predecessor. Sometimes the appearance of criticism is hard to avoid because a major change agenda implies that things were not working as well as they should have in the past. However, criticizing the past can appear self-serving and hurtful to the staff who have worked hard to move the institution to its current position. It is best to focus on forward momentum and opportunities without criticizing the staff or the former CEO. Keep your focus on the positive future you are working to create.

PERSONAL CREDIBILITY

"Credibility is essential to mobilize the energy of employees. But it's hard to build, easy to lose, and difficult to regain."[35] People want to get behind someone they think has the expertise, consistency, values, and legitimacy to succeed with the big vision they have presented. Staff want predictability in their leader, which means a person who is fair and values-based in their decision-making. Remember, people are watching you like hungry hawks, and they want to see that you show up as the same person, regardless of context and whom you are working with.

Know that even before you have arrived, people will already have formed some kind of opinion of you. The intense world of print and broadcast media, coupled with social media, makes it hard not to have a robust digital profile on the internet. You will start your new role with a reputation. You, however, get to decide whether you will reinforce their understanding of you or create something new. The decisions you make and the actions you take in your first six months will have a larger impact than at any other time during your tenure. Even simple acts can become larger stories.

During lunch at the staff canteen on my first day at the National Gallery, instead of sitting at the small elite leadership table, I took my food and sat at the long "drop-in" table for staff. Nobody had seen the director eat there in recent memory. Even though the canteen was sparsely occupied, this small act became a story that made it all around the building—and all the way to New

York City by the end of the day—and I occasionally still hear about it. The same gesture would not be noticed five years into my tenure.

We are often our worst enemy in constructing personal credibility, especially since so many of us have "imposter syndrome." Although this syndrome is common, it is at its most acute when we start new jobs because as we stand at the juncture of a new role, we lose sight of our many past successes.[36] Imposter syndrome can lead to anxiety, self-doubt, and guilt. Knowing that it is a common feeling in new leadership roles, you must work hard to mitigate the feeling. As Oliver Burkeman notes, "The solution to the imposter syndrome is to see that you are one . . . Humanity is divided into two: on the one hand, those who are improvising their way through life, patching solutions together and putting out fires as they go, but deluding themselves otherwise; and on the other, those doing exactly the same, except that they know it. It's infinitely better to be the latter . . . Remember: the reason you can't hear other people's inner monologues of self-doubt isn't that they don't have them. It's that you only have access to your own mind."[37]

THE RISKS

Ciampa and Watkins list the following traps into which people assuming a new leadership role may fall into:

- Getting behind the learning curve
- Being isolated
- Coming in with the answer
- Sticking with the existing team too long
- Attempting to do too much
- Being captured by the wrong people
- Falling prey to the successor syndrome[38]

NOTES

1. Neff and Citrin, *You're in Charge—Now What?* 14.
2. George Bradt, "Follow This Nobel Prize Winner's Advice as an Executive Onboarding into a New Role," August 9, 2017, https://www.forbes.com/sites/georgebradt/2017/08/09/follow-this-nobel-prize-winners-advice-as-an-executive-onboarding-into-a-new-role/?sh=5f21904a6d1d.
3. "Action, and Action Now: FDR's First 100 Days," Franklin D. Roosevelt Presidential Library and Museum, National Archives and Records Administration, accessed February 27, 2024, https://www.fdrlibrary.org/documents/356632/390886/actionguide.pdf/07370301-a5c1-4a08-aa63-e611f9d12c34.
4. "Action, and Action Now: FDR's First 100 Days," Franklin D. Roosevelt Presidential Library and Museum.

5. Franklin D. Roosevelt, "Oglethorpe University Address," May 22, 1932, Fox Theatre, Atlanta, Georgia, https://publicpolicy.pepperdine.edu/academics/research/faculty-research/new-deal/roosevelt-speeches/fr052232.htm.
6. Feiler, *Life Is in the Transitions*, 169.
7. Feiler, *Life Is in the Transitions*, 173.
8. Feiler, *Life Is in the Transitions*, 173.
9. Ciampa and Watkins, *Right from the Start*, 20.
10. Ciampa and Michael Watkins, *Right from the Start*; Bradt, Check, and Pedraza, *The New Leader's 100-Day Action Plan*.
11. Dan Ciampa, "After the Handshake: Succession Doesn't End When a New CEO Is Hired," *Harvard Business Review*, December 2016, https://hbr.org/2016/12/after-the-handshake.
12. Bradt, Check, and Pedraza, *The New Leader's 100-Day Action Plan*, 23.
13. Ciampa and Watkins, *Right from the Start*, 6.
14. Quoted Goldsmith, *What Got You Here Won't Get You There*, 43.
15. Goldsmith, *What Got You Here*, 21.
16. Goldsmith, *What Got You Here*, 21.
17. Ciampa and Watkins, *Right from the Start*, 32.
18. Carolyn Dewar, Martin Hirt, and Scott Keller, "The Mindsets and Practices of Excellent CEOs," McKinsey & Company, October 25, 2019, https://www.mckinsey.com/capabilities/strategy-and-corporate-finance/our-insights/the-mindsets-and-practices-of-excellent-ceos.
19. Bryant, *The Leap to Leader*, 195.
20. Hubert Joly, with Caroline Lambert, *The Heart of Business: Leadership Principles for the Next Era of Capitalism* (Boston: Harvard Business Review Press, 2021); Brené Brown, *Daring Greatly: How the Courage to Be Vulnerable Transforms the Way We Live, Love, Parent, and Lead* (New York: Penguin, 2012).
21. Scott Haber, "Highlighting Your Vulnerabilities—a Strength of a Weakness?" LinkedIn, May 13, 2016, https://www.linkedin.com/pulse/highlighting-your-vulnerabilities-strength-weakness-scott-haber/.
22. Emma Seppälä, "What Bosses Gain by Being Vulnerable," *Harvard Business Review*, December 11, 2014, https://hbr.org/2014/12/what-bosses-gain-by-being-vulnerable.
23. Kate Murphy, *You're Not Listening: What You're Missing and Why It Matters* (New York: Celadon Books, 2020).
24. Murphy, *You're Not Listening*, 137–39.
25. Murphy, *You're Not Listening*, 63.
26. Guy Itzchakov, "Why Listening Well Can Make Disagreements Less Damaging," *Psyche*, February 19, 2024, https://psyche.co/ideas/why-listening-well-can-make-disagreements-less-damaging.
27. Murphy, *You're Not Listening*, 166.
28. Neff and Citrin, *You're in Charge—Now What?* 8.
29. Nitin Nohria, "How New CEOs Establish Legitimacy," *Harvard Business Review*, June 7, 2023, https://hbr.org/2023/06/how-new-ceos-establish-legitimacy.
30. Peter Drucker, "Managing Oneself," *Harvard Business Review*, January 2005, https://hbr.org/2005/01/managing-oneself.
31. Joly, *The Heart of Business*, 110.

32. Joly, *The Heart of Business*, 113.
33. President Franklin D. Roosevelt at the dedication of the National Gallery of Art, Washington, D.C., March 17, 1941.
34. Ciampa, "After the Handshake."
35. Ciampa and Watkins, *Right from the Start*, 119.
36. Kess Eruteya, "You're Not an Imposter: You're Actually Pretty Amazing," *Harvard Business Review*, January 3, 2022, https://hbr.org/2022/01/youre-not-an-imposter-youre-actually-pretty-amazing.
37. Burkeman, "The Eight Secrets."
38. Ciampa and Watkins, *Right from the Start*, 36.

8

The Next Six to Twelve Months

STRAP IN!

In the new CEO's first six months, they have been practicing deep listening, asking questions, meeting people, getting to know the community, gauging the team, and scanning the opportunities and challenges ahead. They have presented an outline of an initial plan to the board and staff and are ready to add substance to the plan. The second six months is where things really start to cook—a steady change agenda coupled with an influx of talent, focused on an exciting future. This is the period to build momentum and readiness for change. You are not just painting the lobby; you are acquiring new furniture and constructing a new doorway.

DEMAND FOR A VISION

"What is your vision for this organization?" is one of the questions a search committee asks a candidate during the first interview. It's such a tough question because nobody can have an authentic vision until they have spent a lot of time listening, thinking, seeing, reading, and learning about an organization, its community, and its audience. In fact, they are asking a candidate for their thoughts about the organization's potential, and they are usually looking for something that reaffirms what they love about it while enlarging the impact and suggesting new possibilities. Still, it can be annoying to be asked repeatedly for your vision when you cannot even find your way to the mailroom. Resist the pressure to unveil a detailed future vision until you are ready.

In the first year, the CEO will likely have developed a personal vision for the organization. They develop a sense for the place, the people, and its potential. While the vision is built upon their listening and learning journey, it is largely developed alone. With fresh eyes and sitting in the catbird seat, the CEO is uniquely positioned to determine an exciting future course for the organization. This is why the search committee selected them over other candidates.

When you are good and ready, start to solicit feedback from trusted advisors about your thoughts and ideas around the organization's exciting future. You can test and refine concepts and ideas, even if you don't yet know quite how they all fit together. You want to socialize the vision with trustees and senior leaders before unveiling it widely to internal and external audiences.

BUILDING TALENT

In his influential book, *Good to Great*, Jim Collins argues that great leaders prioritize talent before all else. He notes that you need to have the right people on the bus, sitting in the right seats on the bus, and the wrong people off the bus, even before you know where you are going or how to get there. Collins states that "great vision without great people is irrelevant."[1] I would argue that you need both because it is hard to attract great people unless you have a compelling opportunity to offer them.

It is usually clear early on if the organization has any profoundly poisonous personnel. These are the people who aren't simply mediocre or disengaged; they are ones who, for whatever reason, actively work to undermine leadership decisions and derail the organization. They are the proverbial "bad apples" who seek to recruit others to their rot. Don't waste any time trying to reform or convince these folks; take immediate action.

The most important and the most difficult part of building talent is figuring out the leadership team. The new CEO needs to work quickly to assess the skills and abilities of the people they have inherited, especially considering the new leader's sense of the needs of the organization at this moment. Some changes happen quickly as people who are opposed to change and the ideas of new leadership select themselves out of the organization, by their choice or otherwise. All leaders need a leadership team they can trust and who will put the organization above their own self-interests, but it takes time to determine whether those people are already in place.

The challenge is that speed matters—as pointed out by Collins, it's hard to move forward without great people, and the new CEO is under real pressure to move fast. That pressure sometimes produces mistakes, and the wrong person is hired for the wrong seat on the bus. In these situations, the CEO must face up to the mistake and correct it quickly. It is human nature to want to ignore a mistake or hope that it resolves itself. It's just harder to acknowledge a mistake when you are new and everyone is watching your every move. But you can't wait.

Most new leaders work to give the senior team that they inherit a chance to prove themselves. The challenge is finding the right performance period because it helps nobody to keep an employee with mediocre performance or who cannot pivot to a new agenda. A new CEO can afford to retain mediocrity even less than someone who has been in the saddle for a while.

> The new leader will not be held responsible for an inherited team's performance during the transition period, but after that its performance is very much her problem. —Ciampa and Watkins, *Right from the Start*[2]

The leadership team members you inherit are the most vulnerable employees you have. They usually know that a new CEO may want to bring some of their team with them and/or establish their own team. They are also not sure that they will want to remain with the new CEO or pursue new initiatives. This uncertainty makes them anxious, and they often have one foot testing the doorway. An emotionally aware CEO senses this, and it complicates the trust, and relationship-building that is underway.

When Hubert Joly took over Best Buy, he focused immediately on building the best leadership team. Working with executive coach Eric Pliner, Joly learned that he needed not only the best leaders, but the best leadership team. Pliner told him, "The best teams are A teams, not collections of A players."[3] Developing the leadership team is not simply about the people you hire, but how they work together as a team. It is the CEO's job to ensure that the team functions as an A team, and this takes a lot of intentional effort.

Once you have your leadership team more or less figured out, you need to focus on the next level down. "Talent is the value creator. Every leader depends on it. It affects business opportunities, business models, strategies, customer acquisition, and strategic execution."[4] Ideally, within the new CEO's first eighteen months, they will have made their key strategic hires in the leadership team and the next level down.

REFINING THE EARLY PLAN TO A STRATEGIC FRAMEWORK

In this second phase, the CEO begins to pull together threads, including their background research, their listening sessions, input from the community, successful early wins, and their talent strategy, to develop a plan to take the organization through the next few years. They should identify the burning imperative of the moment, which will get everyone focused on and aligned around the short-term platform. "The burning imperative is a clear, sharply defined, intensely shared, and purposefully urgent understanding from all of the team members of what they are 'supposed to do now,' and how this burning imperative works with the larger aspirations of the team and organization."[5]

To be successful, the leader needs to align talent, strategy, behavior, and accountability around a shared purpose. New leaders sometimes inherit ambitious plans that are partway along and need to be completed, such as a building project or capital campaign. If this is the case, the leader's plan will be a strategy to execute on the plan they have inherited. Or if the dashboard warning light was on at arrival, the leader will necessarily be focused on triage and rescue. But for most of us, we inherit a great opportunity for new directions and big plans.

CHESTERTON'S FENCE: DON'T DESTROY WHAT YOU DON'T UNDERSTAND

Assuming the new CEO arrives without a burning platform, by this point they should have spent a lot of time trying to understand their predecessor's strategy. It can be tempting for new leaders to try to throw out previous initiatives—and this is sometimes the right call. It is important, however, to interrogate the projects and plans the leader has inherited. Not only is the process helpful in understanding the organization, but it also helps the new leader think through what is known as "second order thinking," i.e., thinking not just about the consequences of the decision, but about the consequences of the consequences. A concept known as "Chesterton's Fence" is based on the idea that when a new leader or innovator encounters a symbolic fence or gate in a road, the first impulse is to just tear down the fence. Chesterton argued in 1929 that it is better to take the time to understand why the fence was erected in the first place. Once you have understood the rationale of the fence and the consequences for either keeping it or tearing it down, it can be dismantled. If you don't work to understand the reason, however, you run the risk of future unanticipated consequences. You should assume that whatever the program or project that you want to eliminate was established for a clear reason, even if the rationale is no longer relevant. Just be sure you understand the potential unintended consequences of eliminating things.[6]

Mark Gumz, the former CEO of Olympus Corporation, advises new leaders that they need the skills to "merge into traffic," noting that if you come onto the highway at 80 miles an hour, you will cause an accident.[7] He is referring to people who come into a new leadership role and immediately make changes, without doing all the advance research, listening, and planning, who are unable to read the room and consider the unintended consequences of poorly thought-out change, while merging into traffic.

MISSION, VISION, AND VALUES

With a significant amount of background under their belt and some momentum, the new leader can now consider whether the institution needs to revise its stated mission, vision, and values. This will be the most important strategic work to do in the first year. I have never inherited an organization that has had all these elements already in place, so it may be a relatively clean slate.

Nevertheless, the period after new leadership is implemented is an excellent time to "kick the tires" and see whether the institution's current mission, vision, and values statements are the correct ones to take into the future.

I love the internal process of grappling with mission, vision, and values. It produces some of the most important conversations a new leader can have with the staff and board about purpose, passion, and desired impact. The process of getting to statements can be nearly as important as the statements themselves. As much as I love the process, I hate the final act of writing the statements because stakeholders want to keep adding more and more words so every idea and thought expressed is included. When I arrived at one museum, the mission statement was a page long and included footnotes. Its length and complexity made it utterly unusable. Leadership needs to remain firm and, once a concise and effective statement has been written, resist the pressure to keep tacking on phrases to please everyone.

Remember, the CEO is ultimately the person who must be happiest with the final statements, as they will use them more than anyone else in the organization. Assuming the institution's mission is aligned with the leader's personal mission, these two statements give the new leader a powerful set of tools to win hearts and minds. Compelling and well-articulated mission and vision statements will enable the CEO to sell the institution, engage funders and stakeholders, and attract talent.

Even if the institution's mission is not changing, it may be healthy to restate it. Mission statements written more than a decade ago tend to focus on the activity of the nonprofit, describing the everyday work of the staff. For museums, mission statements generally declare an intention to collect, preserve, exhibit, and educate. Today, museum mission statements generally focus less on the activities and outputs (collecting, preserving, educating, creating exhibitions) and more on the outcomes and impacts this work will produce (critical thinking, joy, understanding, new perspectives, empathy, shared humanity, concern for the environment, curiosity, etc.). When I arrived at the National Gallery, our mission was "to collect, preserve, exhibit, and foster understanding of works of art." Nothing was untrue or wrong about that statement, but it was largely focused on the staff and our work, and it didn't address the public we served or the difference we wanted to make. We harnessed the opportunity to restate our mission with a focus on public service and the impact we want to make on others. The Gallery's new mission reads: "The National Gallery of Art serves the nation by welcoming all people to explore and experience art, creativity, and our shared humanity." We did not change the actual work that we do in service of our mission, but we changed the way it was stated so that it was outward-facing and impactful.

I cannot overstate how hard it is to remain succinct. People are eager to include every activity and every reason for the institution's existence in the statement. But the longer, dryer, and more complicated a mission becomes, the harder it is to inspire others. A mission statement should describe the organization's purpose and why it exists. I always try to adhere the "Four Ms of a Mission" rule and believe that mission statements should be:

- Memorable
- Motivational
- Manageable
- Measurable

A challenge of developing a vision statement is that most people do not understand the difference between vision and mission statements. Mission statements describe the organization's daily purpose and objectives, while a vision statement describes the future you want to create—and one you may never actually achieve. Vision statements should be aspirational, inspirational, and particularly concise. This is the future you are all working hard for, and it must pack a punch. A vision statement does not describe purpose, strategy, goals, or values, but it should be consistent with all those elements.[8] Boards can be uncomfortable with the lofty vision statements of nonprofits, so the CEO may need to push them. A vision statement reflects, at least in part, the vision of the CEO, but it is owned by the entire institution. The need for brevity means that it is a sound bite for the vision. There is a time and place for a longer description of what the vision means operationally for the organization. The CEO should be rigorous in ensuring that the work produced reflects their vision and understanding of the organization at this moment and that it will enable them to sell that vision more widely, both internally and externally. If the statements don't work for you, go back to the drawing board.

I have always been partial to the *Star Trek* illustration of the difference between a mission and vision:

> *Star Trek* Mission:
>   To explore strange new worlds; to seek out new life and civilizations; to boldly go where no man has gone before.
> *Star Trek* Vision:
>   Space: the final frontier.

It has never been more important for an organization to define and codify its values. In today's VUCA world, leaders rely on agreed-upon values to make large and small decisions. As we are bombarded by unforeseen challenges and new scenarios, our values are there to guide us. Institutional values also enable an organization to develop a healthy shared culture. The creation of new mission, vision, and values statements should involve staff input, but it is most critical to have broad participation from staff in the creation of the institution's values. Mission and vision statements can be harder for people to understand,

and they certainly cannot be drafted by a committee. But values are widely understood, and people feel wonderfully passionate about them.

When we solicited institution-wide input on our values at the National Gallery, we saw the highest survey participation in recent memory. I find our values more meaningful because they were developed by our staff and reflect our collective values. At the National Gallery, our institutional values include:

- Integrity
- Diversity, equity, access, and inclusion
- Excellence
- Deepening public understanding
- Curiosity and continuous learning
- Agility and responsiveness
- Empathy and generosity of spirit

All these values came directly from the staff, with the exception of "empathy" and "generosity of spirit." Because I care so much about these qualities and because generosity is reflected in every part of the National Gallery's history and present operations, I felt strongly about adding it—director's prerogative.

THE STRATEGIC FRAMEWORK

Equipped with the mission, vision, and values, a new CEO is ready to start serious work on a strategic direction. Hopefully, during the first six months, they have painted the lobby, started down some strategic paths, and celebrated several quick wins along the way. Nonprofit CEOs sometimes resist starting a strategic plan in their first year because the sector still clings to the outdated idea that the organization needs a comprehensive, multiyear long-range plan. The pressure from trustees to create five- to seven-year strategic plans shortly after arrival should be resisted, especially in this early phase. As the CEO settles into the role, and begins to make exciting hires, and as trustees and donors feel energized, new opportunities will emerge. My strategy has been to create a kind of "starter" strategic framework for the first few years and then transition into a more formal and longer-term strategic plan.

Creating a type of strategic framework within the first eighteen months, however, is imperative. Don't wait for everything to be settled and perfect. If the organization hired the right CEO, they will be eager to move forward with new initiatives and plans. People need to see how these projects fit together with existing work and where the institution is headed. Without a clear structure for the work, staff and trustees can feel adrift. A strategic framework offers another opportunity for staff and trustee engagement, although the path ahead should be rather clear if the CEO has spent their first six months productively. What are the risks in this strategy, and how might they be mitigated?

What could go wrong? How will we measure our success, and what is the time frame for the work?

A good place to start is to consider a theory of change, outlining the problem you are trying to solve. What are the actions and resources you will need to create the change you want to see? Do you have the right data points? Whom are you serving currently, and whom do you want to serve going forward? What should the program look like to serve your constituents? What resources and partners will the organization need? Who are your competitors and who are your potential collaborators? What barriers might you encounter along the way?

Even if they inherited a solid strategic plan, the new CEO will still want to ask these questions of the current plan and consider some pivots or adjustments. Don't worry if the cover of the plan says it is a five- or ten-year plan, it can be modified and improved. You should look at it with your educated, but fresh perspective and consider the new context in which the organization finds itself. The more time that you allow to pass without making a strong imprint on the strategy, the harder it will be going forward, particularly as new relationships develop that impede impartiality.

COALITION BUILDING

It is well-known in the world of change leadership that in bringing people along, leaders should not focus much of their time on the believers who are already on board, or the disgruntled naysayers. The best place to use your influence is on the people in the middle who haven't decided yet. New CEOs need coalitions of enthusiasts to get the work done. In developing your coalitions, you will need to navigate internal politics, institutional culture, and basic technical challenges (structures, technological capabilities, policies, etc.). Not everyone will come along, and some people will need to be moved out and others adjusted to different roles so that they cannot block the change.

Not everyone needs to like the change a new leader brings, but they do need to understand it. Giving lots of information, clear guidance, and opportunities for skill development will help to bring people along. If they understand the change and can see how their career will develop, they are more likely to get on board, whether they agree with the change or not.

Bradt, Check, and Pedraza divide stakeholders into four camps:

- Committed: people who are on board, driven by the purpose, and ready to roll up their sleeves. Already allies.
- Contributors: people who are new to the organization or role and feeling things out but are eager to be a part of the change. They should be allies.
- Watchers: people who are not drivers for change, but also not harmful. They will do what needs to be done, but they won't advance the cause.
- Detractors: people who perceive a threat to their status or are completely disengaged. If actively hostile, move them out quickly.[9]

CULTURE

> Culture eats strategy for breakfast. —Peter Drucker[10]

Drucker's famous quote reminds us that you cannot do great things as a leader unless you focus on institutional culture. All workplaces have a culture; it is the sum of the values, history, norms, and emotional environment of the institution. Culture is the collective way the organization feels, acts, and expresses itself.

There are three parts to a culture strategy: You must understand and define the current culture; describe the optimal future culture you want to create; and work a plan to forge the desired future culture. There are many ways to tackle institutional culture, and one of the most enduring is known as "the Culture Web," created in 1992 by Gerry Johnson and Kevan Scholes.[11] They defined the elements that make up an institutional culture: institutional stories about the people and events from the past that form part of the institution's lore; rituals and routines of the workplace; symbols (such as logos); organizational structure; control systems; and power structure.[12] Using this framework is a helpful way to create a picture of the current culture.

The next step is to use a similar framework to design the culture that you would like to see to achieve your strategic goals. Comparing the current culture to the desired culture will reveal the gaps between the two and help you focus on the work ahead. You should also identify the barriers and sticking points that need to be resolved and create an action plan. The good news is that you don't have to do this by yourself; culture plans are a good way to engage a group of staff members who are invested in the organization's future (the "committed" and the "contributors"). Employees care about how it feels at the office and are excited to be part of changing the paradigm.

Regardless of how you approach your work on institutional culture, it should be grounded in the organization's values. A culture plan will help articulate the way that values impact behaviors, decision-making, and strategy. For your optimal future culture to be impactful, the institution needs to embrace it by making it a part of all staff communications, rewarding those who demonstrate the culture, and offering constructive feedback to those who need it. When the culture becomes mature, you can also use it as an aid in hiring people who are more likely to succeed in the organization.

COMMUNICATION

> Never give people a void. Just don't, because instinctively they'll think something is awry. —Geoff Vuleta[13]

You simply cannot communicate often enough; use every opportunity and every channel to do so. Keep repeating the most important things: mission, vision, values, culture, and strategy. Repeat them so often it feels awkward and overly repetitive. If trustees and staff hear you referencing these elements frequently, they will understand how important they are and internalize them. I once called a local nonprofit that was one of our museum's collaborators because I needed to confirm their mission statement for a grant application. I was passed around the building and ended up speaking with five people and never got a real answer. This was a leadership failure.

The best way to enable staff and trustees to understand your strategy is to keep it simple and concise. There are always places for detail in the tactical implementation parts of the plan. In your presentations with staff and board, be clear and inspirational. I once presented my transformative strategy to the board and did so with great excitement and energy. But I included far too much detail about the implementation of the strategy and quickly lost the trustees who became stuck on minor tactics. I came away feeling deflated, and they were none the wiser about the exciting big picture. Adam Bryant and Kevin Sharer refer to a CEO's superpower as "simplifying complexity."[14] Keep reminding your audience of the big idea and why it matters.

Dinesh Paliwal, former CEO of Harman International, always took the board a one-page business strategy. The document included the top-line goal in one sentence and described the three actions they would take to get there. He identified the three challenges and told them how they would measure success in a year.[15]

MODEL A LEARNING ORGANIZATION

Museums project themselves as educational institutions—meaning that we educate other people. I like to stress that we are also an institution that learns. A humble CEO who projects curiosity and demonstrates a radical commitment to learning will help the staff during the journey of change under a new leader. Employees need time to reflect, research, and think—activities that are increasingly hard to do in our noisy, digital world. In *Harvard Business Review*, Professor David Garvan wrote, "In the absence of learning, companies—and individuals—simply repeat old practices. Change remains cosmetic, and improvements are either fortuitous or short-lived."[16] As noted in chapter 1, it is the responsibility of the CEO to ensure that employees are given the necessary resources and access to learn and grow. There are so many ways for an organization to embed learning, including reading groups; research forums; brown-bag lunch discussions; casual talks with outside experts; watching online courses together; and subsidized university courses, to name just a few. Encouraging the delivery of regular and honest feedback institution-wide is the best way to model a learning organization.

In chapter 5, I wrote about psychologist Carol S. Dweck's description of the attributes of fixed and growth mindsets.[17] In her research, Dweck has found that organizations can also model these mindsets. Companies with fixed mind-sets embody the thinking that employees "have it" or they don't. They develop only a handful of employees seen as the top talent. These companies are less likely to support risk-taking and innovation. Growth mindset organizations, on the other hand, incorporate employee growth and development into their business plan, and employees feel empowered and committed. Dweck describes fixed mindset organizations as a "culture of genius" and growth mindset organizations as a "culture of development."[18]

We have all heard the phrase that "insanity is doing the same thing over and over again and expecting different results." Likewise, you cannot expect staff members, however talented they may be, to produce great results in areas in which they have no skills or experience if you don't encourage learning and create a structure for the new knowledge to be implemented and shared. As David Garvin observes, learning institutions ensure they become "adept at translating new knowledge into new ways of behaving."[19] At several institutions I have led, we have implemented open-ended staff learning and travel grants, enabling staff across the entire museum to design research trips to expand their thinking about their work. A key requirement of the grant was to share learnings at all staff meetings so other people could learn from their experience and witness the benefits of self-directed learning. At the same time, we developed a culture and format that celebrated both the successes and failures from experimental practice. If you want people to learn, grow, and behave differently, they will certainly take some risks along the way. The institution should celebrate the learnings from failures as well as successes.

In his book, *Where Good Ideas Come From: The Natural History of Innovation*, Steven Johnson argues that the stereotype of the lone genius who suddenly has singular "eureka" moments is a fallacy.[20] Johnson observes that good ideas usually blossom in an ecosystem of collaborative structures, in broad social networks, and in places that encourage collaboration. He praises "liquid networks" as the places where people with different expertise and divergent ideas come together with a similar goal, often serendipitously. Sometimes these good ideas occur by chance but within innovative networks. Finally, he points out that the best environments for good ideas are also ones that allow for and are punctuated by error.[21]

EXPECT TO BE TESTED

> During your first year there will never be a time when your strategic agenda isn't being criticized, questioned, and debated. —Neff and Citrin, *You're in Charge, Now What?*[22]

New leaders must have tough skins. It's hard work, filled with grueling hours, a lot of pressure, and intense scrutiny. The first year is difficult, for corporate and nonprofit leaders, for people new to the CEO role and for those with years of experience. Every time I write a congratulations card to someone taking over a new leadership role, I remind them that the first year is rarely a lot of fun. The good news is, it keeps getting better and better after that first year.

Remember that the first year is not always fun for the staff, either. It is inevitable that when a new leader arrives, they worry about their future with the organization. They are still trying to figure out whether they trust this new person and if their arrival will benefit them. Several months into one of my tenures, I felt a lot of anxiety and decided to call the employee assistance program hotline. After I said that I was calling from the museum, the receptionist said, "Oh, we are getting a lot of calls from there these days. There's a new leader making a lot of changes, and everyone is anxious." I felt terrible and declined to make an appointment. That phone call was a memorable low point.

WHEN TO TAKE A STAND

In your first year, you may encounter some real moments of discord, when you question your comfort at the organization. These are the moments to double down on your values and the institution's values to navigate difficult waters. There may be times when you have to step up to the "I may not be the right person for this job" precipice. If you find yourself in this position, think long and hard and don't act quickly or when driven by emotion. I have tottered on this precipice just a couple of times, and it was always because of a moral issue that I felt dictated a very clear response and it took some time to get the board to my position on the matter. While these moments can happen at any time, they happen more often in the first year of a job change because a new leader sometimes discovers shortcuts or problems about which the board was either unaware or looked the other way. Sometimes you need to take a stand, and it may cost you your job. Being a courageous leader means you are willing to take that risk, and being a savvy leader means you know the extremely rare moment when it is warranted. Become adept at pausing with deep breaths and thinking things through.

NOTES

1. Collins, *Good to Great*, 41–42.
2. Ciampa and Watkins, *Right from the Start*, 24.
3. Joly, *The Heart of Business*, 157.
4. Anish Batlaw and Ram Charan, *Talent: The Market Cap Multiplier* (Washington, D.C.: Ideapress Publishing, 2022), 5.
5. Bradt, Check, Pedraza, *The New Leader's 100-Day Action Plan*, 98.
6. Johnny Thompson, "How 'Chesterton's Fence' Can Help You Avoid Terrible Decisions," Big Think, November 16, 2023, https://bigthink.com/business/chestertons-fence/.

7. Bryant, *The Leap to Leader*, 73.
8. Ciampa and Watkins, *Right from the Start*, 169.
9. Bradt, Check, Pedraza, *The New Leader's 100-Day Action Plan*, 31-32.
10. Peter Drucker, *Classic Drucker: Essential Wisdom of Peter Drucker from the Pages of Harvard Business Review* (Boston: Harvard Business Review Press, 2006).
11. Gerry Johnson, Richard Whittington, and Kevan Scholes, *Fundamentals of Strategy* (London: FT Press, 2011).
12. Johnson, Whittington, and Scholes, *Fundamentals of Strategy*.
13. Geoff Vuleta, "Corner Office: Can You Handle the 100-Day To-Do List?" interview by Adam Bryant, *New York Times*, November 20, 2010, https://www.nytimes.com/2010/11/21/business/21corner.html.
14. Adam Bryant and Kevin Sharer, *The CEO Test: Master the Challenges That Make or Break All Leaders* (Boston: Harvard Business Review Press, 2021), 11.
15. Bryant and Sharer, *The CEO Test*, 21.
16. David Garvin, "Building a Learning Organization," *Harvard Business Review*, July-August 1993, https://hbr.org/1993/07/building-a-learning-organization.
17. Dweck, *Mindset*, 3-14.
18. Dweck, *Mindset*, 142.
19. Garvin, "Building a Learning Organization."
20. Steven Johnson, *Where Good Ideas Come From: The Natural History of Innovation* (New York: Riverhead Books, 2010).
21. Johnson, *Where Good Ideas Come From*, 43, 129-46.
22. Neff and Citrin, *You're in Charge*, 132.

9

The First-Time CEO and the Internal Candidate

THE INTERNAL CANDIDATE

Even if the board is enthusiastic about an internal candidate, they should still do a robust professional search. If the candidate is the right one, they will only look stronger to everyone after the committee sees other candidates. Ultimately, a successful internal candidate will have more support from staff, board, and stakeholders if they triumphed in a fair and rigorous process. Promoting a candidate from within without a proper search can also lead to resentment and accusations of a lack of transparency, so it is better to avoid the situation altogether.

The insider has both advantages and disadvantages. Obviously, they already know the organization and the players. If they are a viable candidate, then they must also have a good idea of the opportunities and challenges ahead and a vision for how the institution can best serve its mission. There are, however, several challenges an insider has that an external candidate does not. The insider rarely has the impartial and clear view of the organization's strengths and challenges.

I have seen many inside candidates struggle to describe an exciting future that is not simply a slight variation of the present. They are so close to the operation that it is hard for them to rise and look at the organization from a new perspective. In counseling internal candidates, I always tell them they have the hardest job of all the candidates, since boards think they already know them. When Alan Lacy was selected to be the CEO of Sears, he had served for six years as the chief financial officer at the company. He advises that new leaders coming from the inside take the time to become "an outsider," working with an external facilitator and seeking input from internal experts.[1]

Boards should treat internal candidates with care and will want to set out guard-rails to protect the employee, maintain confidentiality, ensure fair consideration, and provide safety if they are ultimately not selected. If the committee is working with a search consultant, that person should be the sole contact for the internal candidate. Committees need only interview fully qualified internal candidates, and they should go through the exact same screening and interview process as all other candidates.

Internal candidates can be particularly tricky when a donor of great influence serving on the committee has their favorite internal candidate. I have seen cases where the search consultant and the entire rest of the committee thinks the patron's candidate would be a disaster, and they struggle between the decision of potentially upsetting the patron and losing their financial support or hiring a terrible CEO. Clearly, the committee must not hire a terrible candidate, but it doesn't make the situation any easier for the committee members who must navigate the awkward situation. In these cases, you should interview the patron's favored candidate, but be firm and never hire the wrong person just to make a donor happy. Doing so is a violation of the board's fiduciary duty, and it never ends well for the board, the candidate, or the donor.

APPOINTING AN INTERNAL CEO

When an insider is selected, the staff may perceive that the future is "business as usual." As Dewar, Hirt, and Keller point out in "The Mindsets and Practices of Excellent CEOs," ". . . data also show that externally hired CEOs are more likely to move with boldness and speed than those promoted from within an organization. CEOs who are promoted from internal roles should explicitly ask and answer the question, 'What would an outsider do?' as they determine their strategic moves."[2]

Another potential drawback is that the staff may feel as though they know the internal candidate, which can be both good and bad. When I was promoted from curator to director at the age of twenty-eight in Fresno, California, the move from being a colleague to the boss was a jolt for all of us. The museum had virtually ground to a halt as the staff had united in their distrust of the former CEO. Frustration and negativity united the staff, not positive forward momentum. Suddenly, he was gone, and so was the crutch. When I took over, I noticed that a senior staff member, a former collegial friend, was arriving at ten in the morning and departing at three in the afternoon most days. And her performance had suddenly become my problem. It is hard for most people to move from friend to boss. Constant complaining about the former director had replaced the museum's mission and become our motivation and collegial cohesion. You need to be prepared for the new relationship that you will have with former colleagues and peers as you move from friend and colleague to respected leader.

Inside candidates don't get the benefit of a real "honeymoon period" because people think you know the organization and that they know you. As a new leader, they now need to be strategic about identifying advisors and confidants. It is hard not to rely on former associations and friendships, but keeping these close associations in your new role may make other staff members feel anxious and left out. You want to be seen as fair and balanced in your approach as possible to the entire staff, so approach your relationships as though it is a clean slate.

A new leader who was an internal candidate needs to be thoughtful about the differences between them and their predecessor and how they will communicate both differences and similarities. What programs, projects, and initiatives will you continue, and which will you stop? How will you engage the staff and listen with "new ears" to their perspective on the organization you already know so well? How will you create your new CEO agenda? It is natural to feel a sense of loss because you no longer have the job that you knew well and in which you felt comfortable and competent. Internal candidates can also feel a loss of control—which is true! As the CEO, you are no longer able to have your fingers so deeply inside a single pie, let alone in a whole organization of many pies. You cannot be involved in everything, and that takes getting used to.

I was a new CEO, a peer-turned-boss, I had negligible leadership experience, and the museum was facing a financial crisis. Only a twenty-eight-year-old would be naïve enough to take on a challenge like that. I vividly recall being confronted with daily decisions and having no experience (or internet) to draw upon. I used intuition and my gut to make decisions daily. The good news is that intuition served me well, and I still use it today, but I am happy to now have experience to reference.

THE FIRST-TIME CEO

Some of the surprises for new CEOs arise from time and knowledge limitations—there is so much to do in complex new areas, with imperfect information and never enough time. Others stem from unexpected and unfamiliar new roles and altered professional relationships. Still others crop up because of the paradox that the more power you have, the harder it is to use.[3] —"Seven Surprises for New CEOs," *Harvard Business Review*

The most important question someone interested in leadership can ask themselves is, "Do I really want to lead? Why?" Just because you are a star performer in your field or because it is the next likely step in your career, shouldn't be the reason. Leadership isn't for everyone and being an excellent fundraiser, curator, CFO, or administrator doesn't mean that you will be an excellent leader. Star subject experts don't necessarily make great leaders, and the role is not an honorary award for a career well served. Someone thinking about moving into leadership should really interrogate the impulse and be sure that it doesn't stem from the desire for money, power, or a title. A Heidrick & Struggles study of twenty thousand global corporate searches revealed that a sobering 40 percent of the leaders hired failed or quit within eighteen months.[4] These are really hard jobs, and you can only make it if the challenge of leadership excites and energizes you and you are prepared for a long learning journey.

Governance experts Richard Chait, William Ryan, and Barbara Taylor observe that the field of nonprofits has moved from nonprofit administrators to organizational leaders, noting that trustees expect "far more of nonprofit CEOs today than a genial personality, moral probity, managerial acumen, and passionate commitment to the organization's social mission. Stakeholders, in a word, expect *leadership*."[5] Transitioning from management to leadership requires a complete mindset shift as the work and the necessary skills to perform the job are different. In his excellent article about this shift, Michael D. Watkins outlines seven "seismic shifts" a person needs to make as they move into leadership: specialist to generalist; analyst to integrator; tactician to strategist; bricklayer to architect; problem solver to agenda setter; warrior to diplomat; supporting cast member to lead role.[6] Leadership means that you are no longer helping people to execute tasks, but empowering them and helping them to see new perspectives so they can advance to new heights. Your work is about helping other people to do what they love, to succeed, and to win the glory.

Remember that we all have behavioral blind spots about ourselves that we do not see, but others do. The best way to manage them is to ask for feedback from other people. Build your network of trusted advisors and solicit honest and specific feedback about your strengths and weaknesses. I know so many people who have failed as they made the move from management and subject specialism to leadership because they were not aware of their own skill and interest gaps, and they lacked the curiosity to learn about themselves and the role of leader before accepting a job.

I mentor several emerging and new CEOs, and I have great empathy for what they go through. They have all the challenges and learning curves that any new tenure brings, but they are simultaneously learning how to be a leader at scale. When interviewing first-time CEO candidates, I always ask them to consider the areas where they are weak and/or have little interest or experience, noting that leadership requires so many different skills that nobody can be good at all of them. Candidates are loathe to say that they will need help in anything. It's a poor response in an interview because leaders should demonstrate self-awareness and humility. A new director should be honest with themselves and others about the parts of the job in which they have little skill or interest and are therefore not as effective. If you know your weaknesses, you know to hire others with those strengths.

The leadership consulting firm RHR International has found that first-time CEOs are often too slow to make changes in their leadership team.[7] They hesitate and don't trust themselves enough, and they are prone to giving more benefit of the doubt than experienced CEOs. New CEOs don't have the template for analyzing senior talent, and they probably don't have robust Rolodexes with the names of talented people they have worked with in the past.[8]

It is harder for young women to navigate this early period as they have two challenges—being young and being female. After serving as director of the museum in Fresno for three years, I interviewed for a slightly larger museum. At the end of the interview, the board chair told me that I was "far too young and far too female" for their curators to report to me. They hired a former football player instead. First-time women leaders are sometimes monitored more closely than first-time male leaders by trustees, and they are more likely to be told that they should find an executive coach and seek out sartorial advice. Early in my tenure at one institution, a trustee said to me, in front of other trustees, "things would go better if you would do as you are told." This trustee ended up being one of my biggest supporters because I earned his respect over time. Younger women are just less likely to start with the respect usually ascribed to the role due to the sexism addressed in chapter 6.

I highly recommend incorporating formal leadership training as you embark on your first few years as a CEO. Engaging an executive coach is a great option, and many out there specialize in a variety of fields. There are also some terrific leadership books available (see the bibliography). Many universities offer excellent executive education programs, and I have benefited from several. They tend to be expensive and difficult for nonprofits to afford, but I have found that generous donors who are invested in you will often readily step up to help. If you are unsure where to look, tap your network to find the resources you need.

Boards need to understand the risk involved in hiring a first-time CEO and be aware of their new leader's steep learning curve. Obviously, I am here to say that it can be done, but boards need to know that it is their job to support this first-time leader.

OPEN SEASON

> When you're managing a division or a department or a project, you've got someone above you to whom you can refer—or defer—big decisions . . . That's the biggest difference between being the head of a division of a company and becoming the CEO. Every heartbeat, every murmur, gets reported on, whether it's about the company, about you, or about things that are happening in your life. Everything becomes open season. That's yet another aspect of the job to get prepared for during the countdown period. —Neff and Citrin, *You're in Charge, Now What?*[9]

New leaders will learn that trustworthy information becomes difficult to obtain. The information that reaches you is filtered through several layers of interpretation and self-interest. You learn that you are not only trying to access information, but you also must try to parse and interpret it, deciding whom and what to trust.

New leaders need to establish legitimacy. Nitin Nohria distinguishes between authority-based leadership (based on formal power); competence-based leadership (focused on performance); and legitimacy-based leadership (based on actions that inspire trust).[10] Nohria compiled the six behaviors a first-time leader should cultivate and exhibit:

- Communicate clearly
- Demonstrate fairness
- Behave with integrity
- Put the organization first
- Stay grounded
- Maintain and express a sense of purpose[11]

First-time CEOs find they need to use their time differently in this new role. Assuming they have experience as senior managers running a division or department, they are accustomed to focusing their time on the day-to-day management of the people and operations of that division. But the demands on a leader's time are completely different, moving between internal and external stakeholders, managing a board of trustees, fundraising, participating in community activities as a leader, etc. A new leader must decide what to let go of in their new role, and they will likely have to let go of much of the work that propelled them into this new leadership role. Finally, it is hard to manage time to balance the new role and family life. As one CEO commented, "In the end, there is no such thing as [life] balance. There are only trade-offs."[12]

WORKING WITH A BOARD

First-time CEOs have it especially tough. Most likely, they will have gotten used to leading leaders in their previous roles and have proven themselves by managing down. But, if they are the senior most executive in the company reporting to the owners or board, they are going to have to spend at least 25% of their time managing up (board and shareholders) and at least 25% of their time managing external stakeholders like community leaders, collaborators, and the press. That means they will be able to spend less than 50% of their time managing down—a dramatically different proposition. —George Bradt in *Forbes*[13]

Welcome to the new reality of not having just one boss, but lots and lots of bosses! Trustee management is a huge part of a nonprofit CEO's job, and it will consume a lot of your time and emotional energy. You need to develop a keen political awareness to understand what happens in board-rooms, as people jockey for power and influence. First-time CEOs have it especially tough, as they are probably used to spending most of their time managing down. In a leadership role, they will spend at least half their time working with the board and donors, leaving much less time for internal operations.

My advice for working with trustees for first-time directors:

- You are generally only as good as the last thing the trustees heard. While we live and breathe our work, they are busy people and often forget what you said in a meeting two months ago.
- When you really need the vote of a difficult decision to go a certain way, don't go into the meeting without having your votes already lined up.
- Remain in close communication with your board chair and never surprise them. It is always worth it to take the extra time to walk them through a situation in advance.
- When introducing a new initiative, program, or project that people could be on the fence about, arrange in advance for a few of your most influential trustees to step up as soon as the presentation finishes and enthusiastically endorse the project.
- You can be overwhelmed by trustees' "good ideas" that are often not so helpful and are make-work for the staff. All you need to do is smile and say, "Thank you." If you hear the same idea three times, you may need to investigate it. Don't chase every suggestion that comes your way, or you won't have time for the important things.
- Develop a keen eye for coalitions. They can work for and against you.
- Make sure you always have a professional annual review. Feedback is always good, and it is a safeguard for you.
- Be authentic and communicate your values.
- Never forget that no matter how rich and successful your trustees are, they probably don't know your industry like you do. Own your sector expertise and don't be afraid to educate people.
- As frustrating as it is, and no matter how deep your expertise, boards often give greater credence to an "outside expert," so use them strategically.
- While it is inevitable that you develop a close relationship with board members, remember that they are not your peers and not your friends. Twenty years ago, an experienced museum director told me never to forget that to your trustees, you are just the hired help. He was right, and I have never forgotten it.

My advice for board members working with a first-time director:

- Remember that this new director is not the same person and does not have the experience of your previous director.
- When interviewing, aspirational directors often exaggerate their experience and skill level; it's natural to do so. Be aware that there will be skill and experience gaps and support your CEO's learning journey.
- Consider the risks your new director faces and minimize them. Risks can be a new community; new industry; increased operational scale; inheriting unhappy stakeholders, structural deficits, disgruntled employees, etc.
- Be a mentor. Shortly after I was appointed to my first directorship, one of our younger trustees called me into the hall after a committee meeting. He noted that he was also a young leader, stressed his support, and offered to be helpful in any way. I appreciated that he didn't talk down to me and felt reassured by his confidence in me.
- There is a steep learning curve—be patient and constructive.
- Invest in your leader by helping with a professional development plan, formal onboarding, and coaching. Even better, pay for some of their courses.
- Know the difference between support and micromanagement.
- The best question I have ever received from a trustee was the one who would call me regularly and ask, "What's worrying you? How can I help?"

Finally, one of the best pieces of advice I received as a young, new director was to get out in the community and ask people for their advice. It's human nature—most people love being asked for their advice—and as a result, people become invested in your success. You will have friends and supporters for the rest of your career if you follow this advice.

IT IS COLD AT THE TOP OF THE MOUNTAIN (CHINESE PROVERB)

It's true, many leaders suffer from feeling isolated. For me, the greatest stress comes from the hard decisions that impact staff—unavoidable layoffs, job reassignments, performance improvement plans, etc. These responsibilities can be slightly easier when you are in your first six months because they feel less personal, but they are also harder because you haven't yet built up trust from the staff. No matter how you look at it, however, having to make difficult decisions that impact peoples' livelihoods and careers is often the worst part of being a leader. It is particularly difficult for internal candidates because your former in-house network is now your employee base, and you must keep a certain distance in your new role. You don't want to expose yourself to accusations of favoritism, and sharing your difficult leadership decisions can compromise both you and the employees.

Grow and nurture your network. I have been carried through my career on the shoulders of so many wonderful and supportive colleagues from other museums and nonprofits, as well as an amazing husband who is an excellent source of leadership advice based on observations of human behavior. To counteract isolation, solicit input across the institution and use your network, ensuring that you listen to diverse points of view. Executive coach Naz Beshati suggests leaders create a "silent advisory board," (i.e., another leader, a mentor, or a coach who will listen to you talk through tough decisions, thoughts, and emotions as a confidant.)[14] Leaders are prone to burnout, stress, and depression, so watch for the signs and do not hesitate to get help. Prioritize healthy habits like exercise, hobbies, and friendships since they not only make you feel better, but they also enable you to fulfill your leadership potential. Earlier in my career, when I was single, I would come home at night emotionally drained by looking after other people all day long. I would look at my cat, Maude, and say, "what are *you* going to do for *me*?"

NOTES

1. Neff and Citrin, *You're in Charge*, 45.
2. Dewar, Hirt, and Keller, "The Mindsets and Practices of Excellent CEOs."
3. Michael E. Porter, Jay W. Lorsch, and Nitin Nohria, "Seven Surprises for New CEOs," *Harvard Business Review*, October 2024, https://hbr.org/2004/10/seven-surprises -for-new-ceos.
4. Brooke Masters, "Rise of a Headhunter," *Financial Times*, March 30, 2009, https://www.ft.com/content/19975256-1af2-11de-8aa3-0000779fd2ac.
5. Richard P. Chait, William P. Ryan, Barbara E. Taylor, *Governance as Leadership: Reframing the Work of Nonprofit Boards* (Hoboken, NJ: Wiley, 2005), 3.
6. Michael D. Watkins, "How Managers Become Leaders," *Harvard Business Review*, June 2012, https://hbr.org/2012/06/how-managers-become-leaders.
7. Sarah Green Carmichael, "Who New CEOs Fire First," *Harvard Business Review*, July 8, 2013, https://hbr.org/2013/07/who-new-ceos-fire-first.
8. Carmichael, "Who New CEOs Fire First."
9. Neff and Citrin, *You're in Charge*, 42.
10. Nohria, "How New CEOs Establish Legitimacy."
11. Nohria, "How New CEOs Establish Legitimacy."
12. Porter, Lorsch, and Nohria, "Seven Surprises for New CEOs."
13. George Bradt, "Stop Hiring First-Timers. Let Them Learn at Someone Else's Expense," *Forbes*, January 9, 2024, https://www.forbes.com/sites/george-bradt/2024/01/09/avoid-hiring-first-timers-let-them-learn-at-someone-elses -expense/?sh=3835f8826ede.
14. Naz Beheshti, "Is It Truly Lonely at the Top?" *Forbes*, September 26, 2018, https://www.forbes.com/sites/nazbeheshti/2018/09/26/is-it-lonely-at-the-top/?sh =6eb1a5a969c5.

10

The Dream Job

Fortune sides with he who dares. —Virgil

When I was twenty years old, I flew to Rome by myself, leaving home to partici- pate in a two-month archeological dig in central France, followed by six months of study in Rome. I had to make my way around Rome to leave a suitcase at my school and then find a night train to Paris. From Paris, I took another train to Clermont-Ferrand in central France, and the next day I took a local bus to a tiny village in France's Massif Centrale. It was a complicated itinerary, and I was all on my own.

I will never forget my arrival in Rome's Termini train station. It is a chaotic place, and I was accosted by men offering taxi service (among other things). I was lonely, afraid, and forced to make quick decisions on my feet. If I could have walked through a magic doorway back into the safety of my childhood bedroom, never to leave home ever again, I would have gladly done so. Since this wasn't an option, I found my, way and my journey, and its many conse- quences, are part of the story that has shaped my life and made me who I am today. Fortune sided with me because I dared.

Career changes—especially the ones that uproot and challenge you— are frightening, and one can come up with a host of reasons, many of them legitimate, to stay put. I urge people to be honest with themselves as they draw up their pros-and-cons list of a career move, as fear can be disguised in any number of excuses. Often, a new job and a move can result in increased quality-of-life circumstances, such as better schools, improved standard of living, proximity to family, a more challenging job, etc. In addition, pushing our- selves into a new position helps us to grow into better leaders. In the spirit of the adage, "what doesn't kill us makes us stronger," a professional "life quake" (Bruce Feiler) can help to forge a stronger and more experienced person and professional since the skills needed to manage a successful transition expand our leadership potential and help us to grow.[1] Absent other factors, prioritize enlargement over comfort.

The job of a museum director is one of privilege in so many ways. One of the greatest privileges I enjoy is that thirty years in, I am still on an expansive learning journey. I relish the benefit of learning assiduously about art, history, and culture. In leadership roles, you learn more about yourself, the people around you, and the human condition. I have worked with hundreds of trustees during my career and have learned so much from many of them. Nonprofit leaders are wasting a golden resource if they are not learning from the free advice of trustees, colleagues, and stakeholders.

MY BIGGEST TAKEAWAYS ON THIS INTERIM PERIOD FOR CEOS

1. CEOs need to be planful about their future and the organization's future.

    Nobody enjoys succession planning, but it is critical. You owe it to your organization to create a professional succession plan; they are not hard to do, and there are many templates out there. To maximize a succession plan and the organization's success, implement a leadership development program across the organization.

    Career opportunities often seem like they come about as a combination of luck and happenstance. While this might be true of the opportunity itself, your position and readiness for the appointment are on you. Develop your career by developing yourself; embrace curiosity and own your own learning journey. Work hard to understand what motivates you and brings you joy; we succeed most fully when we feel the work we do enlarges us and gives us energy.

2. Do your homework on every opportunity that you seriously consider.

    Don't forget that boards rarely know what is really going on, and unless *you* do proper due diligence, you will start your new tenure with the words, "I just had *no* idea how bad things are here." At the end of the day, it's your responsibility to do the research. Forewarned is forearmed.

3. Use the interim period to prepare for your new role.

    Don't waste your transition time. As much as possible, turn your focus from your current role to planning for your future job. If the change requires a relocation, take care of your family, and prioritize the decisions that will make the physical move easier for everyone. Learn about your new community and plan for your first one hundred days.

    Don't forget to plan for the emotional part. Being new all over again is draining, especially when you are leaving a successful operation. Remember that you are starting all over again almost at ground zero with your new staff, and you will be earning credibility. People are watching and judging every word that you say and every change that you make—and that is stressful.

4. Arrive ready to "paint the lobby."

 Arrive onsite ready to maximize your first year. Listen, learn, and plan. Be decisive and ensure a series of small wins—and don't forget to celebrate victories along the way. Have a detailed plan for your first six and twelve months in the job, remembering that you cannot do it alone, so assemble talent. (This is easier to do when you are always recruiting.)

5. Be prepared for the emotional and physical challenges of the first year.

 You will have plenty of low points and exhaustion after a CEO transition, so don't forget the best piece of advice I was given—give it a year. You simply cannot cut short the time it takes for you to prove your credibility, learn the short-term pitfalls and opportunities, create a plan, and successfully navigate unforeseen challenges. Celebrate your first-year anniversary with a vacation and look after yourself.

MY BIGGEST TAKEAWAYS ON THIS INTERIM PERIOD FOR BOARDS

1. Leverage the moment to understand the institution and its future possibilities.

 Boards rarely know how the nonprofit organization really runs and what its strengths, weaknesses, and opportunities are. This is your golden chance to do so. But don't just look at past performance; consider the uncertain future and dream a bit. Invest the board's time and resources in getting the transition right.

2. Keep the main thing the main thing: find a great leader.

> Leadership is about inspiring, enabling, and empowering others to do their absolute best together to realize a meaningful and rewarding shared purpose. —George B. Bradt, Jayme A. Check, and Jorge E. Pedraza, *The New Leader's 100-Day Action Plan: Take Charge, Build Your Team, and Deliver Better Results Faster*[2]

 At the end of the day, boards simply need to hire great leaders. Now, finding a great leader may not be so simple, but if trustees remain laser-focused that the goal is to find a great leader, it will cut down the noise. I have heard it all: "we must have someone who understands our community"; "we just need a great fundraiser"; "we have to have someone who will be a 'good fit' with the staff"; "the candidate must have a PhD"; "the new director must have gravitas"; "the new CEO must have experience running a food pantry our size or larger"; etc.

 In *The CEO Test*, Adam Bryant and Kevin Sharer write that after years of interviews, they believe that CEOs who are successful are those who can write and communicate a simple plan, build cultures and manage teams, drive change, and navigate crises.[3] Your search committee will likely have its own leadership criteria; whatever it is, be deliberate about hiring candidates who demonstrate they can do it.

3. Watch out for unintended bias.

    In their discussions, search committee members will bring biases to the table that we all have; it's a given. The important thing is for committee members to know that it happens and to watch for it in themselves and others. Remember that it is everyone's responsibility and not just that of the committee members who are diverse (in gender, sexuality, race, ethnicity, disability, etc.).

4. The problem is often the board. Be courageous.

    Even after suffering numerous revolving-door directors, I have heard trustees say, "We have a really great board" without acknowledging that a big part of the institution's leadership problem is a result of governance problems. Who else will own and fix governance dysfunction if not the board? If a board cares at all about the organization (and if they don't, this is a good time to leave), this transition period is the best time to resolve internal problems—but it takes courage, as it often means confronting peers.

5. Search committee members will be the sought-after repositories of frustrations and dreams.

    Expect to be chased into public restrooms and taken out to lunch by other trustees and stakeholders who want to tell you their priorities for the next leader. The interim period is the time for everyone to express displeasure about how the last leader handled something they care about. They will lobby you for the prioritization of their favorite program or initiative. Listen, smile, and say thank you.

When I first conceived of this book, I thought I was writing about how to hire a nonprofit CEO and how CEOs might navigate their first year in a new organization. I soon realized I was simply writing a leadership book that was focused on a specific point in a CEO's and an organization's life cycle. It is a vulnerable time, filled with both great opportunity and many potential pitfalls. Since beginning the book, I have encountered many nonprofit CEOs and volunteers struggling to navigate their way through a nonprofit transition, and these transitions seem to be occurring more frequently. CEOs and trustees need to become adept at transition, and I hope this book and some of the sources listed help others navigate their way to a safe landing.

In the final verses of Canto XXXIV of *The Inferno*, Dante and Virgil climb along a path by a stream and emerge out of hell together. It has been a long journey since they started out in the dark wood. As they climb out of an opening in the cave, they emerge into a bright world of the night sky illuminated by stars and are no longer lost.

NOTES

1. Feiler, *Life Is in the Transitions*, 94–95.
2. Bradt, Check, and Pedraza, *The New Leader's 100-Day Action Plan*.
3. Bryant and Sharer, *The CEO Test*.

Appendix: A Menu of My Favorite Interview Questions (compiled over a decade)

GENERAL

- Tell me how your education and experience led you to this particular opportunity that we are discussing today.
- What do you enjoy the most about what you do? The least?
- What gets you up in the morning? What motivates you?
- What are you really good at, but would rather not do anymore?
- Please tell us about a project you found meaningful. Why was it meaningful to you? What does this success say about you?
- What can you accomplish here that you couldn't do anywhere else?
- What kind of mandate would you like from the board?
- At the end of your career, what kind of achievement do you want to be remembered for?
- What are you personally passionate about?

MANAGEMENT

- How many people do you currently manage? What is the hardest part of management for you?
- Can you tell us about a time that you resolved a difficult HR issue? How did it go? What did you learn along the way?
- In your experience, what are the main challenges change-makers face while trying to proceed with a radical innovation/change?
- What's your specific strategy for collaboration within and across divisions?
- How will you go about assessing the talent already onboard?
- How will you stimulate new thinking and debate across the institution?
- How do you support the growth of your staff—managers and mentors—both short-term and across their career? How do you nurture new leaders?

- Talk about your experience diversifying your staff. Can you quantify the difference? How did you get there?
- How would you balance the immediacy of putting out day-to-day unexpected fires with the need for a longer-term strategy? How you manage your time and energy?
- How do you ensure that your direct reports are growing the teams' skills and leadership competencies?
- How would you handle a situation in which you needed expertise (yourself or on your team) that you don't have?
- How would you go about breaking down siloes in your division—and across the institution?
- Tell us about your communication style.
- What metrics do you use to measure and reward success?
- What are your techniques for attracting high-quality talent to an organization?
- Describe the most difficult person you've ever had to deal with in a work situation. How did you manage that relationship?

LEADERSHIP

- Who are you as a leader? What is your leadership philosophy? What actions do you take that demonstrate that philosophy?
- How would a staff member describe your leadership? What about the board?
- Tell us about your experience creating and working with a strategic plan.
- Please share key leadership lessons you have learned from watching other leaders.
- Give examples for the ways that you manage a talent strategy in your organization? How do you develop leaders?
- What is your strategy for staying out of the details and micromanagement? As a leader, what do you give up?
- Please tell us about a time when you had to make a difficult or unpopular decision. What was the process? How did you come to your decision?
- Tell me about an accomplishment that shaped your career.
- How should an effective CEO spend their time?
- From what you know about us, what do you anticipate would be your immediate top strategic priorities?
- How will you inspire the board and staff to fulfill your vision?
- Please describe a time when you used your leadership skills to overcome a challenging situation.
- What areas of your life are you trying to enhance to become a more-well-rounded leader?

DIVERSITY, EQUITY, ACCESS, AND INCLUSION

- Describe one or two specific activities or programs you have created to promote diversity, equity, and/or inclusion in your current job?
- What diversity challenges have you faced?
- Please share with us your definition (or understanding) of each of these terms: *diversity*; *equity*; and *inclusion*.
- What challenges have you faced when it comes to DEI?
- What are your specific inclusion strategies for your direct reports? How do you ensure that the whole organization experiences a culture of inclusion?
- What do you think is the most challenging aspect of working in an inclusive environment?
- What steps are you taking to eliminate bias in your hiring process?
- What is your sense of the complexities and leadership challenges related to social justice and multiculturalism?
- Describe a specific situation in which you encountered a conflict with a person from a different cultural background than yours. How did you handle the situation?
- Can you describe a time when you dealt with a staff member or colleague who was being culturally insensitive, racist, ableist, sexist, or homophobic?
- How have you incorporated the viewpoints and perspectives of underrepresented groups into your work?
- Give an example of a time when you had to expend social capital to champion diversity and inclusion.
- Describe a situation in which you utilized your multicultural skills to solve a problem.
- Tell us about a time when you changed your behavior after being exposed to perspectives that were different from your own.
- Describe your experience or explain how you have been educated to understand the history of African Americans, Latinx/Hispanics, Asian Americans, Native Americans, and other historically marginalized communities.

ENVIRONMENTAL SUSTAINABILITY

- Please tell us how you have incorporated sustainability into your work.
- Describe three to four sustainability strategies you might implement here. What KPIs would you use?
- How do you engage stakeholders in your sustainability work?
- Tell us about an initiative that didn't go as planned. What challenges did you face, and how did you resolve them?
- How would you go about embedding ESG in our operations?

- How do you keep up with the latest trends, best practices, and data in sustainability?
- What are the potential threats you see in the next five years to our field, and what should we be doing to guard against them?

THOUGHTS SPECIFIC TO THE ORGANIZATION

- Assuming you have read our 990, what specific observations do you have about our financial position?
- What do you think we do not do well, but could be known for?
- Who do you think is our competition?
- What can you accomplish here that you couldn't do anywhere else?
- How is the role of the museum (or another type of organization) changing in the twenty-first century?
- How do you think about the role of social media and content strategy in the field?
- How do you stay abreast of current thinking in the field?
- How will the field be different in a decade?
- What professional lessons have you learned during the COVID-19 pandemic? Would you have done anything different if you knew in March 2020 what the crisis would entail?
- How might your work fuel curiosity in our audience, besides the traditional functions of exhibitions and publications?
- Why do art museums matter?

CULTURE FIT

- Describe your ideal colleague. How do you work with your colleagues?
- How do you define *organizational culture*?
- Please describe your ideal organizational culture. How would you help us to get there?
- Describe how you have overseen cultural change to help drive innovation.
- What principles guide your career?
- Describe the culture at your current place of employment. How have you played a part in creating it?
- Please give us an example of a time when you were able to change an institution's culture.

FOR INTERNAL CANDIDATES

- What thing would you like to change about how people in your division work together?
- How would you break down our siloes?

- How will you elevate our strategic priorities?
- Are there one or more of our institutional values that really resonate with you?
- Staff in the institution have suggested a reorganization. How would you approach that?
- How will you scale up with a handful of direct reports to over X?
- How will you move from being a peer to being the boss?
- How would you go about making unpopular calls?
- If employees could choose the leader, would they choose you? Why? How do you know?

CRITICAL THINKING AND CURIOSITY

- If you received twenty-five million dollars to solve a global problem, what issue would you address and how?
- What do you know about our organization? What do you think our reputation is? (Be honest.)
- What are the societal trends that could disrupt us? What are you keeping your eye on?
- How many footballs could fit in this room? How would you figure it out?
- In your current (or most recent) role, what kinds of problems do you help solve on a daily basis?
- How might AI impact our business in the next five years?
- What are our biggest opportunities in the next five years?
- What have you read recently? (You want to find out if candidates read actively beyond their field.)
- Describe a hypothetical situation and ask the process they would use to resolve it, including what information they would want to know. Are they able to put the question into a context? How do they consume and synthesize different pieces of information? What immediate steps would they take?
- Have you ever found yourself unable to stop learning about something you'd never encountered before? Why? What kept you persistent?

QUESTIONS TO DEMONSTRATE EMOTIONAL INTELLIGENCE

- What life events have made you the person you are today? How did you become the person you are?
- What is something that people often get wrong about you? Why is that? Are there times when it is true?
- What did you learn about *yourself* during the COVID-19 global pandemic?
- Describe your ideal co-worker. (People tend to describe themselves.)
- Describe a time when you became aware of your own bias.

- What is one of the most difficult pieces of feedback you have received? How did it cause you to change?
- We all have weaknesses. What are yours, and how have you worked to improve them?
- What motivates you at work?
- Have you received feedback you didn't agree with? What did you do about it?
- Tell us about a time when you had to deliver negative feedback. How did you approach the situation?
- How do you handle failure? How do you recover from it?
- Can you tell us about a time when you had to work with a team that included people you didn't particularly like?
- What sort of behavior annoys you? What are your triggers?
- What mechanisms do you use in your professional life to get feedback?
- What mechanisms do you use to illuminate your blind spots?
- Give an example of how you walk in the shoes of people we serve and those with whom we work.
- How does your own identity impact your work with a diverse staff?
- As you look back across your life to date, is there a central theme? If you drew a symbol to summarize your life, what would it be?
- No leader is great at everything; what are your weaker areas? How do you manage your weaknesses?
- Tell us about one or two of your biggest failures. What did you learn about yourself?
- How would you describe your reputation in the field?
- What techniques do you use to read the effect that your behavior has on other people?
- How do you handle burnout?

COURAGE

- What is the scariest leadership decision that you have had to make?
- All leaders make poor hires from time to time. Can you tell us about a time when you made a hiring mistake? When did you realize it? How did you resolve the situation?
- Please describe your philosophy around risk.
- What is the biggest risk you have taken in your life?
- What was the most unpopular decision you made at your current workplace?
- Was there a time when you strongly disagreed with a board directive (or the decision of a supervisor)? How did you resolve it?
- Tell us about a time when you overturned the status quo.

- What is the most difficult situation you have faced, and how did you show courage in it?
- How do you develop courage in yourself?
- Tell us about a time when you faced adversity and how you handled it. What did you learn from it?
- What keeps you up at night?

CHANGE MANAGEMENT

- What strategies would you use to identify opportunities and the need for change across the organization?
- Can you describe in detail a change initiative that you were a part of, one you were accountable for leading? Describe the key stakeholders that you had to engage, what you did on your own, what you did through or with others, what the inputs were versus the outcomes, etc.
- How would you engage stakeholders in your change management plan? What would buy-in look like?
- How would you assess the impact of the proposed change and measure your success?
- In leading major change initiatives, what are different ways that you have overcome the natural tendency of most people to resist change?
- How would you assess risk?
- How would you handle failure?
- Can you give us an example of a major change initiative you led in the past?
- What strategies would you use to motivate the staff in the change process?
- What is your approach in setting long-term goals for the institution?
- Tell us how you use data to make decisions.

VALUES

- What three to four values are most important to you as a leader? How do you demonstrate them? Can you give examples of how you used them in your decision-making?
- What is the role of values in decision-making?
- How have you lived those values professionally?
- Why are your values important in your success?
- How would someone who works for you describe your leadership to someone else?

CREATIVITY/OUT-OF-THE-BOX THINKING

- Tell me about something you have invented (in either your personal or your professional life).

- Where do you find inspiration for your work?
- What has been your most creative solution to a problem you have confronted?
- What do you need in an employer to enhance your creativity?
- Can you describe any unconventional solutions you have developed to solve a problem?

FINAL QUESTIONS

- What question did we not ask you today that we should have?
- What are the three main things you want us to remember about our conversation?

Acknowledgments

The greatest privilege afforded by my 30-year career as a museum director is the gift of continuous learning. Artists, works of art, history, and human creativity continue to stimulate my curiosity. I am lucky that my learning journey has included the history of art as well as the art and science of leadership.

I have had the opportunity to learn from a number of great leaders on the boards of the four museums I have directed. I hold deep appreciation for the volunteers who step forward to lead art museums in America; trustees have always been partners in my work. The time, talent, and resources that trustees invest in our institutions due to their belief in the power of art to improve lives and foster community inspires me. I want to thank the men and women who served with me as board chairs and presidents and who have taught me so much about leadership throughout my career: Richard Johansen, John Horstmann, Cathy Frost, Thomas Stern, Henry Doggrell, William Deupree, Kevin Adams, Mike Fryt, Brian Palmer, Diane Lilly, John Himle, Hubert Joly, Maurice Blanks, Nivin MacMillan, Rick Beinecke, Sharon Rockefeller, Mitch Rales, and David Rubenstein. Working alongside these accomplished leaders has been an honor.

At the National Gallery, I want to thank Michele Nichols, chief of staff, who has also taught me so much during our 17 years of working together. I could not have completed this project without the diligence of Celina Emery, our brilliant Strategic Initiatives Manager. With her project management, research abilities, and editorial skills, Celina is a valued partner in much of my public-facing work.

Finally, I am forever grateful to my dear husband, Jim Lutz, for supporting my career and helping me be a better person. Jim has coached me as I have navigated the challenge of changing jobs, teaching me the lesson at the center of this book's introduction, that most airline accidents happen at take off and landing.

Bibliography

Alighieri, Dante. *The Divine Comedy*. Translated by A. S. Kline. http://www.poetryin-translation.com/.

Armstrong, Karen. *The Great Transformation: The Beginning of Our Religious Traditions*. New York: Knopf, 2006.

Bartelby. "Would You Rather Be a Manager or a Leader?" *Economist*, October 23, 2023. https://www.economist.com/business/2023/10/23/is-being-a-leader-really-sexier-than-being-a-manager.

Batlaw, Anish, and Ram Charan. *Talent: The Market Cap Multiplier*. Washington, D.C.: Ideapress Publishing, 2022.

Beheshti, Naz. "Is It Truly Lonely at the Top?" *Forbes*, September 26, 2018. https://www.forbes.com/sites/nazbeheshti/2018/09/26/is-it-lonely-at-the-top/?sh=6eb1a5a969c5.

Beinart, Peter. "Fear of a Female President." *Atlantic*, October 2016. https://www.theatlantic.com/magazine/archive/2016/10/fear-of-a-female-president/497564/.

Bennet, James. "The Bloomberg Way." *Atlantic*, November 2012. https://www.theatlantic.com/magazine/archive/2012/11/the-bloomberg-way/309136/.

Bertrand, Marianne, and Sendhil Mullainathan. "Are Emily and Greg More Employable Than Lakisha and Jamal? A Field Experiment on Labor Market Discrimination." *American Economic Review*, 94, 4 (September 2004): 991–1013. DOI: 10.1257/0002828042002561.

Bielińska, Inga. "Executive Presence Is Being Reframed in the Modern World." *Forbes*, February 6, 2023. https://www.forbes.com/sites/forbescoachescouncil/2023/02/06/executive-presence-is-being-reframed-in-the-modern-world/?sh=6bc947ee51d5.

Bleiweis, Robin, Jocelyn Frye, Rose Khattar. "Women of Color and the Wage Gap." The Center for American Progress, published November 17, 2021. https://www.americanprogress.org/article/women-of-color-and-the-wage-gap/.

BoardSource. "Term Limits." Accessed February 22, 2024, https://boardsource.org/resources/term-limits/.

Bradt, George. "Follow This Nobel Prize Winner's Advice as an Executive Onboarding into a New Role." *Forbes*, August 9, 2017. https://www.forbes.com/sites/georgebradt/2017/08/09/follow-this-nobel-prize-winners-advice-as-an-executive-onboarding-into-a-new-role/?sh=5f21904a6d1d.

Bradt, George. "Stop Hiring First-Timers. Let Them Learn at Someone Else's Expense." *Forbes*, January 9, 2024. https://www.forbes.com/sites/georgebradt/2024/01/09/avoid-hiring-first-timers-let-them-learn-at-someone-elses-expense/?sh=3835f8826ede.

Bradt, George. "What Harvard Must Do to Onboard Its New President Successfully." *Forbes*, February 2, 2024. https://www.forbes.com/sites/georgebradt/2024/02/02/what-harvard-must-do-to-onboard-its-new-president-successfully/.

Bradt, George B., Jayme A. Check, and Jorge E. Pedraza. *The New Leader's 100-Day Action Plan: Take Charge, Build Your Team, and Deliver Better Results Faster*. Hoboken: John Wiley & Sons, Inc., 2022.

Brait, Ellen. "'Résumé Whitening' Doubles Callbacks for Minority Job Candidates, Study Finds." *Guardian*, March 17, 2016. https://www.theguardian.com/world/2016/mar/17/jobs-search-hiring-racial-discrimination-resume-whitening-callbacks.

Braswell, Porter. "This Is the Difference Between Racism and Racial Bias." *Fast Company*, October 19, 2022. https://www.fastcompany.com/90796690/this-is-the-difference-between-racism-and-racial-bias.

Brown, Brené. *Daring Greatly: How the Courage to Be Vulnerable Transforms the Way We Live, Love, Parent, and Lead*. New York: Penguin, 2012.

Bryant, Adam. *The Corner Office*. New York: St. Martin's Griffin, 2011.

Bryant, Adam. *The Leap to Leader*. Boston: Harvard Business Review Press, 2023.

Bryant, Adam, and Kevin Sharer, *The CEO Test: Master the Challenges That Make or Break All Leaders*. Boston: Harvard Business Review Press, 2021.

Bureau of Labor Statistics. "Employee Tenure in 2022." Accessed August 17, 2023, https://www.bls.gov/news.release/pdf/tenure.pdf.

Burkeman, Oliver. "The Eight Secrets to a (Fairly) Fulfilled Life." *Guardian*, September 4, 2020. https://www.theguardian.com/lifeandstyle/2020/sep/04/oliver-burkemans-last-column-the-eight-secrets-to-a-fairly-fulfilled-life.

Burns, Courtney, Leah Windsor, Gabrielle Peterson, and Allison Sulkowski. "Women World Leaders and the Language of the Political Double Bind." November 2019. https://www.researchgate.net/publication/337316826_Women_World_Leaders_and_The_Language_of_the_Political_Double_Bind.

Burns, Robert. "To a Louse," accessed February 25, 2024, https://www.poetry.com/poem/30592/to-a-louse.

Carmichael, Sarah Green. "Who New CEOs Fire First." *Harvard Business Review*, July 8, 2013. https://hbr.org/2013/07/who-new-ceos-fire-first.

Carville, James. Political Dictionary. https://politicaldictionary.com/words/its-the-economy-stupid/.

Chait, Richard P., William P. Ryan, Barbara E. Taylor. *Governance as Leadership: Reframing the Work of Nonprofit Boards*. Hoboken, NJ: Wiley, 2005.

Chamorro-Premuzic, Tomas. "If Women Are Better Leaders, Then Why Are They Not in Charge?" *Forbes*, May 7, 2021. https://www.forbes.com/sites/tomaspremuzic/2021/03/07/if-women-are-better-leaders-then-why-are-they-not-in-charge/?sh=4116ae756c88.

Chamorro-Premuzic, Tomas, and Cindy Gallop, "7 Leadership Lessons Men Can Learn from Women," *Harvard Business Review*, April 1, 2020. https://hbr.org/2020/04/7-leadership-lessons-men-can-learn-from-women.

Charan, Ram. "The Secrets of Great CEO Selection." *Harvard Business Review*, November 14, 2016. https://hbr.org/2016/12/the-secrets-of-great-ceo-selection.

Christov-Moore, Leonardo, Elizabeth A. Simpson, Gino Coudé, Kristina Grigaityte, Marco Iacobonia, and Pier Francesco Ferrari. "Empathy: Gender Effects in Brain and Behaviour." *Neuroscience and Biobehavioral Reviews* 46, Pt. 4. https://doi.org/10.1016/j.neubiorev.2014.09.001.

Ciampa, Dan. "After the Handshake: Succession Doesn't End When a New CEO Is Hired." *Harvard Business Review*, December 2016. https://hbr.org/2016/12/after-the-handshake.

Ciampa, Dan, and Watkins, Michael. *Right from the Start: Taking Charge in a New Leadership Role*. Boston: Harvard Business School Press, 1999.

Collins, Jim. *Good to Great: Why Some Companies Make the Leap . . . and Others Don't*. London: Random House, 2001.

Covey, Stephen R. *The 7 Habits of Highly Effective People*. New York: Free Press, 1989.

Cunff, Anne-Laure. "Liminal Creativity." Accessed February 9, 2024, https://nesslabs.com/liminal-creativity.

Danao, Monique. "11 Essential Soft Skills in 2024 (with Examples)." *Forbes*, April 20, 2023. https://www.forbes.com/advisor/business/soft-skills-examples/.

Darity Jr., William A., and Patrick L. Mason. "Evidence on Discrimination in Employment: Codes of Color, Codes of Gender." *Journal of Economic Perspectives*, 12, 2 (Spring 1998): 63–90.

Davey, Liane. "The Status Quo Is Risky, Too." *Harvard Business Review*, May 2, 2014. https://hbr.org/2014/05/the-status-quo-is-risky-too.

Detert, James R. "What Courageous Leaders Do Differently." *Harvard Business Review*, January 7, 2022. https://hbr.org/2022/01/what-courageous-leaders-do-differently.

Dewar, Carolyn, Martin Hirt, and Scott Keller. "The Mindsets and Practices of Excellent CEOs." McKinsey & Company, October 25, 2019. https://www.mckinsey.com/capabilities/strategy-and-corporate-finance/our-insights/the-mindsets-and-practices-of-excellent-ceos.

Douglas-McNab, Emily. "Succession Planning 101." *Education Week*, November 6, 2012. https://www.edweek.org/leadership/opinion-succession-planning-101/2012/11.

Dovidio, John. "Understanding Your Racial Biases, with John Dovidio, PhD," in *Speaking of Psychology*. Produced by the American Psychological Association. https://www.apa.org/news/podcasts/speaking-of-psychology/understanding-biases.

Dowd, Maureen. "Lady of the Rings: Jacinda Rules." *New York Times*, September 8, 2018. https://www.nytimes.com/2018/09/08/opinion/sunday/jacinda-ardern-new-zealand-prime-minister.html.

Drucker, Peter. *Classic Drucker: Essential Wisdom of Peter Drucker from the Pages of Harvard Business Review*. Boston: Harvard Business Review Press, 2006.

Drucker, Peter. "Managing Oneself." *Harvard Business Review*, January 2005. https://hbr.org/2005/01/managing-oneself.

Dweck, Carol S. *Mindset: The New Psychology of Success*. New York: Ballantine Book, 2016.

Eagly, Alice, and Linda L. Carli. "Women and the Labyrinth of Leadership." *Harvard Business Review*, September 2007. https://hbr.org/2007/09/women-and-the-labyrinth-of-leadership.

The Economist. "Pity the Modern Manager—Burnt-Out, Distracted and Overloaded." October 24, 2023. https://www.economist.com/business/2023/10/24/pity-the -modern-manager-burnt-out-distracted-and-overloaded.

Edelstein, Sophia. "How to Hire and Interview for a High-Growth Business." *Forbes*, January 17, 2024. https://www.forbes.com/sites/forbesbusinesscouncil/2024/01 /17/how-to-hire-and-interview-for-a-high-growth-business/.

Emmerling, Robert J., and Daniel Goleman. "Emotional Intelligence Issues and Common Misunderstandings." *The Consortium for Research on Emotional Intelligence in Organizations*, October 2003. https://www.eiconsortium.org/pdf/EI_Issues_And_Common _Misunderstandings.pdf.

Eruteya, Kess. "You're Not an Imposter: You're Actually Pretty Amazing." *Harvard Business Review*, January 3, 2022. https://hbr.org/2022/01/youre-not-an-imposter -youre-actually-pretty-amazing.

Eurich, Tasha. "What Self-Awareness Really Is (and How to Cultivate It)." *Harvard Business Review*, January 4, 2018. https://hbr.org/2018/01/what-self-awareness-really -is-and-how-to-cultivate-it.

Feiler, Bruce. *Life Is in the Transitions: Mastering Change at Any Age*. New York: Penguin Press, 2020.

Feldman, Kaywin. "Unpacking 'Gravitas': A Museum Director Reflects on Gender Inequities in the Museum Field." *Museum*, March–April 2017. https://www.aam-us.org/ wp-content/uploads/2017/10/unpacking-gravitas-1-1.pdf.

Fels, Anna. "Do Women Lack Ambition?" *Harvard Business Review*, April 2004. https:// hbr.org/2004/04/do-women-lack-ambition.

Fels, Anna. *Necessary Dreams: Ambition in Women's Changing Lives*. New York: Anchor Books, 2004.

Fernández-Aráoz, Claudio. "The Challenge of Hiring Senior Executives." In *The Emotionally Intelligent Workplace: How to Select For, Measure, and Improve Emotional Intelligence in Individuals, Groups, and Organizations*, edited by Cary Cherniss and Daniel Goleman, 182–208. New York: Wiley, 2003.

Finely, Andrew, Curtis M. Hall, and Amanda Marino. "Negotiation and Executive Gender Pay Gaps in Nonprofit Organizations." *Review of Accounting Studies, Claremont McKenna College Robert Day School of Economics and Finance*. Research Paper No. 338548, March 11, 2021. https://dx.doi.org/10.2139/ssrn.3385848.

Frank, Christopher, Paul Magnone, and Oded Netzer. "How to Evaluate a Job Candidate's Critical Thinking Skills in an Interview." *Harvard Business Review*, September 25, 2023. https://hbr.org/2023/09/how-to-evaluate-a-job-candidates-critical-think ing-skills-in-an-interview.

Franklin D. Roosevelt Presidential Library and Museum, National Archives and Records Administration. "Action, and Action Now: FDR's First 100 Days." Accessed February 27, 2024. https://www.fdrlibrary.org/documents/356632/390886/actionguide .pdf/07370301-a5c1-4a08-aa63-e611f9d12c34.

Frey, William H. "The US Will Become 'Minority White' in 2045, Census Projects." Brookings, March 14, 2018. https://www.brookings.edu/articles/the-us-will -become-minority-white-in-2045-census-projects/.

Fryer, Roland, and Steven Levitt. "The Causes and Consequences of Distinctively Black Names." *Quarterly Journal of Economics*, Vol. 119, No. 3 (August 2004): 767–805.

Fuller, Joseph, and William Kerr, "The Great Resignation Didn't Start with the Pandemic." *Harvard Business Review*, March 23, 2022. https://hbr.org/2022/03/the -great-resignation-didnt-start-with-the-pandemic.

Garry, Joan. "10 Ways Boards Screw Up Leadership Transitions." Joan Garry Consulting, June 27, 2022. https://www.joangarry.com/leadership-transitions/.

Garvin, David. "Building a Learning Organization." *Harvard Business Review*, July–August 1993. https://hbr.org/1993/07/building-a-learning-organization.

George, Bill. "VUCA 2.0: A Strategy for Steady Leadership in an Unsteady World." *Forbes*, February 17, 2017. https://www.forbes.com/sites/hbsworkingknowledge /2017/02/17/vuca-2-0-a-strategy-for-steady-leadership-in-an-unsteady-world/ ?sh=3c1951613d84.

Gerdeman, Dina. "Minorities Who 'Whiten' Job Résumés Get More Interviews." Harvard Business School, May 17, 2017. https://hbswk.hbs.edu/item/minorities-who -whiten-job-resumes-get-more-interviews.

Gino, Francesca. "The Business Case for Curiosity." *Harvard Business Review*, September–October 2018. https://hbr.org/2018/09/the-business-case-for-curiosity.

Goldberg, Emma. "Gen X Is in Charge. Don't Make a Big Deal About It." *New York Times*, July 7, 2023. https://www.nytimes.com/2023/07/07/business/gen-x-in-charge -companies-chief-executives.html.

Goldsmith, Marshall, with Mark Reiter. *What Got You Here Won't Get You There*. London: Profile Books, 2007.

Goleman, Daniel. *Emotional Intelligence: Why It Can Matter More Than IQ*. New York: Bantam, 1995.

Goleman, Daniel, and Richard Boyatzis. "Emotional Intelligence Has 12 Elements. Which Do You Need to Work On?" *Harvard Business Review*, February 6, 2017. https:// hbr.org/2017/02/emotional-intelligence-has-12-elements-which-do-you-need-to -work-on.

Grant, Adam. "The Dark Side of Emotional Intelligence." *Atlantic*, January 2, 2014. https://www.theatlantic.com/health/archive/2014/01/the-dark-side-of-emotional -intelligence/282720/.

Haber, Scott. "Highlighting Your Vulnerabilities—A Strength or a Weakness?" LinkedIn, May 13, 2016. https://www.linkedin.com/pulse/highlighting-your-vulnerabilities -strength-weakness-scott-haber/.

Hewlett, Sylvia Ann. "The New Rules of Executive Presence." *Harvard Business Review*, January–February 2024. https://hbr.org/2024/01/the-new-rules-of-executive -presence.

Hindsman Stacia, PsyD, Robin, and Pardi, Lita. "Address the Need for Nonprofit Succession Planning." BoardSource Blog, July 27, 2016. https://blog.boardsource.org/blog/ address-the-need-for-nonprofit-succession-planning.

Hyman, Jeff. "Why Humble Leaders Make the Best Leaders." *Forbes*, October 31, 2018. https://www.forbes.com/sites/jeffhyman/2018/10/31/humility/?sh =70dc72101c80.

Itzchakov, Guy. "Why Listening Well Can Make Disagreements Less Damaging." Psyche, February 19, 2024. https://psyche.co/ideas/why-listening-well-can-make-disagreements-less-damaging.

James, William. "A World of Pure Experience." *Journal of Philosophy, Psychology and Scientific Methods*, Vol. 1, No. 20 (Sep. 29, 1904), 533–43. https://doi.org/10.2307/2011912.

Jaspers, Karl. *The Origin and Goal of History*. Translated by Michael Bullock. London: Routledge & Keegan Paul, 1953.

Johnson, Gerry, Richard Whittington, and Kevan Scholes. *Fundamentals of Strategy*. London: FT Press, 2011.

Johnson, Stefanie K. "2021 Is a Tipping Point for Female Leaders." Bloomberg, January 31, 2021. https://www.bloomberg.com/opinion/articles/2021-01-31/women-leaders-are-doing-better-during-the-pandemic #xj4y7vzkg.

Johnson, Steven. *Where Good Ideas Come From: The Natural History of Innovation*. New York: Riverhead Books, 2010.

Joly, Hubert, with Caroline Lambert. *The Heart of Business: Leadership Principles for the Next Era of Capitalism*. Boston: Harvard Business Review Press, 2021.

Katz, Michael. "The COVID Crisis Shows Why We Need More Female Leadership." *Fortune*, March 17, 2021. https://fortune.com/2021/03/17/covid-female-women-leadership-jacinda-ardern/.

Keller, Scott. "Reorganizing to Capture Maximum Value Quickly." McKinsey & Company, February 20, 2018. https://www.mckinsey.com/capabilities/people-and-organizational-performance/our-insights/reorganizing-to-capture-maximum-value-quickly#/.

Keller, Scott. "Successfully Transitioning to New Leadership Roles." McKinsey & Company, May 23, 2018. https://www.mckinsey.com/capabilities/people-and-organizational-performance/our-insights/successfully-transitioning-to-new-leadership-roles#/.

Kendall, Shari, and Deborah Tannen. "Gender and Language in the Workplace." In *Gender and Discourse*, edited by Ruth Wodak, 81. New York: Sage Publications, Inc., 1997. https://psycnet.apa.org/doi/10.4135/9781446250204.n5.

Kissel, Neal H., and Patrick Foley. "The 3 Challenges Every New CEO Faces." *Harvard Business Review*, January 23, 2019. https://hbr.org/2019/01/the-3-challenges-every-new-ceo-faces.

Kochhar, Rakesh, Kim Parker, and Ruth Igielnik. "Majority of U.S. Workers Changing Jobs Are Seeing Real Wage Gains." Pew Research Center, July 28, 2022. https://www.pewresearch.org/social-trends/2022/07/28/majority-of-u-s-workers-changing-jobs-are-seeing-real-wage-gains/.

Konish, Lorie. "67% of Americans Have No Estate Plan, Survey Finds. Here's How to Get Started on One." CNBC, published April 11, 2022. https://www.cnbc.com/2022/04/11/67percent-of-americans-have-no-estate-plan-heres-how-to-get-started-on-one.html.

Lakoff, Robin Tolmach. *Language and Woman's Place*. New York: Oxford University Press, 1975.

Lam, Bourree. "When Résumés Are Made 'White' to Please Potential Employers." *Atlantic*, March 23, 2016. https://www.theatlantic.com/business/archive/2016/03/white-resume-diversity/475032/.

Landles-Cobb, Libbie, Kirk Kramer, and Kate Smith Milway. "The Nonprofit Leadership Development Deficit." *Stanford Social Innovation Review*, October 22, 2015. https://ssir.org/articles/entry/the_nonprofit_leadership_development_deficit.

Lanpher, Katherine. "The Conversation: Donna Brazille and Deborah Tannen Discuss Our Hillary Problem." *More*, October 2007.

Levy, Nat. "Microsoft CEO Satya Nadella: It's better to be a 'learn-it-all' than a 'know-it-all'." Geek Wire, August 4, 2016. https://www.geekwire.com/2016/microsoft-learn-it-all/.

Liera, Roman, and Cheryl Ching. "Reconceptualizing 'Merit' and 'Fit': An Equity-Minded Approach to Hiring." In *Higher Education Administration for Social Justice and Equity*, edited by A. Kezar and J. Posselt: 111–31. New York: Routledge, 2019.

López, Ian Hany. *Dog Whistle Politics: How Coded Racial Appeals Have Reinvented Racism and Wrecked the Middle Class*. Oxford, UK: Oxford University Press, 2015.

Luo, Michael. "'Whitening' the Résumé." *New York Times*, December 5, 2009. https://www.nytimes.com/2009/12/06/weekinreview/06Luo.html.

Luscombe, June B. "Jacinda Ardern Helped New Zealand Beat Cornavirus. Next Up: Getting Re-elected." *Time*, June 12, 2020. https://time.com/5852567/new-zealand-coronavirus-jacinda-ardern-election/.

Malik, Stephynie. "Curiosity: A Leadership Trait That Can Transform Your Business to Achieve Extraordinary Results." *Forbes*, August 26, 2020. https://www.forbes.com/sites/forbescoachescouncil/2020/08/26/curiosity-a-leadership-trait-that-can-transform-your-business-to-achieve-extraordinary-results/.

Manpower Group. "The Flux Report: Building a Resilient Workforce in the Face of Flux." Accessed January 24, 2024, https://www.manpowergroup.co.uk/wp-content/uploads/2015/04/The-Flux-Report_whitepaper.pdf.

Masters, Brooke. "Rise of a Headhunter." *Financial Times*, March 30, 2009. https://www.ft.com/content/19975256-1af2-11de-8aa3-0000779fd2ac.

Mehrabian, Albert. *Nonverbal Communication*. New York: Routledge, 1977. https://doi.org/10.4324/9781351308724.

Merchant, Nilofer. "Don't Demonize Employees Who Raise Problems." *Harvard Business Review*, January 30, 2020. https://hbr.org/2020/01/dont-demonize-employees-who-raise-problems.

Mullaney, Tom. "ART: The Museum World's Kingmaker Crowns Again." *New York Times*, April 25, 2004. https://www.nytimes.com/2004/04/25/arts/art-the-museum-world-s-kingmaker-crowns-again.html.

Murphy, Heather. "Picture a Leader. Is She a Woman?" *New York Times*, March 16, 2018. https://www.nytimes.com/2018/03/16/health/women-leadership-workplace.html.

Murphy, Kate. *You're Not Listening: What You're Missing and Why it Matters*. New York: Celadon Books, 2020.

Neff, Thomas J., and James M. Citrin. *You're in Charge—Now What? The Eight Point Plan*. New York: Three Rivers Press, 2005.

Nohria, Nitin. "How New CEOs Establish Legitimacy." *Harvard Business Review*, June 7, 2023. https://hbr.org/2023/06/how-new-ceos-establish-legitimacy.

Novak, David R. "Killing the Myth That 93% of Communication Is Nonverbal." Accessed February 25, 2024, https://davidrnovak.com/writing/article/2020/03/killing-the-myth-that-93-of-communication-is-nonverbal.

Parker, Kathleen. "What Steinem, Albright, and Clinton Don't Get About Millennial Women." *Washington Post*, February 9, 2016. https://www.washingtonpost.com/opinions/what-steinem-albright-and-clinton-dont-get-about-millennial-women/2016/02/09/7d156d80-cf73-11e5-abc9-ea152f0b9561_story.html.

Pew Research Center. "The Data on Women Leaders." September 27, 2023. https://www.pewresearch.org/social-trends/fact-sheet/the-data-on-women-leaders/.

Porter, Michael E., Jay W. Lorsch, and Nitin Nohria. "Seven Surprises for New CEOs." *Harvard Business Review*, October 2024. https://hbr.org/2004/10/seven-surprises-for-new-ceos.

Rayan, Robin. "Ace Your Next Interview Using the STAR Method." *Forbes*, May 5, 2023. https://www.forbes.com/sites/robinryan/2023/05/25/ace-your-next-interview-using-the-star-method/.

Reece, Brian J., Vu T. Tran, Elliott N. DeVore, and Gabby Porcaro, editors. *Debunking the Myth of Job Fit in Higher Education and Student Affairs*. New York: Stylus Publishing, 2019.

Reynolds, Russell. "Global CEO Turnover Index." Accessed February 23, 2024, https://www.russellreynolds.com/en/insights/reports-surveys/global-ceo-turnover-index.

Rifkin, Glen. "Making a Difference; Mr. Olsen Hangs On . . ." *New York Times*, November 10, 1991. https://www.nytimes.com/1991/11/10/business/making-a-difference-mr-olsen-hangs-on.html.

Rohrschach, Kimberly. "Know Before You Go." Center for Curatorial Leadership, June 1, 2017. https://www.curatorialleadership.org/in-the-field/know-before-you-go/.

Roosevelt, Franklin D. "Oglethorpe University Address." May 22, 1932, Fox Theatre, Atlanta, Georgia. https://publicpolicy.pepperdine.edu/academics/research/faculty-research/new-deal/roosevelt-speeches/fr052232.htm.

Roosevelt, President Franklin D., at the dedication of the National Gallery of Art, Washington, D.C., March 17, 1941.

Rost, Joseph C. *Leadership in the 21st Century*. New York: Praeger, 1991.

Sagaria, Mary Ann Danowitz. "An Exploratory Model of Filtering in Administrative Searches: Toward Counter-Hegemonic Discourses." *Journal of Higher Education* 73, no. 6 (2002): 677–710. http://www.jstor.org/stable/1558402.

Salovey, Peter, and John D. Mayer. "Emotional Intelligence." *Imagination, Cognition and Personality* 9.3 (1989). https://doi.org/10.2190/DUGG-P24E-52WK-6CDG.

Sensoy, Özlem, and Robin DiAngelo. "'We are all for diversity, but . . .' How Faculty Hiring Committees Reproduce Whiteness and Practical Suggestions for How They Can Change." *Harvard Educational Review*, Vol. 87, No. 4 (Winter 2017). https://doi.org/10.17763/1943-5045-87.4.557.

Seppälä, Emma. "What Bosses Gain by Being Vulnerable." *Harvard Business Review*, December 11, 2014. https://hbr.org/2014/12/what-bosses-gain-by-being-vulnerable.

Spencer Jr., Lyle M., and Signe M. Spencer. *Competence at Work: Models for Superior Performance*. New York: Wiley, 1993.

Stevenson, Bryan. "The Power of Proximity." YouTube video, 34:15, June 26, 2018. https://www.youtube.com/watch?v=1RyAwZlHo4Y.

Stoller, Joel. "Managing Yourself: Single-Pilot Crew Resource Management." *Flight Training Magazine*, December 5, 2000. https://www.aopa.org/news-and-media/all-news/2000/december/flight-training-magazine/managing-yourself.

Stone, Douglas, and Sheila Heen. *Thanks for the Feedback*. New York: Penguin, 2014.

Sullivan, Paul. "In Philanthropy, Race Is Still a Factor in Who Gets What, Study Shows." *New York Times*, May 1, 2020. https://www.nytimes.com/2020/05/01/your-money/philanthropy-race.html.

Sweales, Jo. "3 Steps to Introduce a Learn-It-All Culture." Microsoft Blog, published January 10, 2019. https://www.microsoft.com/en-gb/industry/blog/cross-industry/2019/10/01/introduce-learn-it-all-culture/.

Tannen, Deborah. "The Double Bind." In *Thirty Ways of Looking at Hillary: Reflections by Women Writers*, edited by Susan Morrison. New York: HarperCollins, 2008.

Tannen, Deborah. "The Power of Talk: Who Gets Heard and Why." *Harvard Business Review*, September–October 1995. https://hbr.org/1995/09/the-power-of-talk-who-gets-heard-and-why.

Tannen, Deborah. "The Self-Fulfilling Prophecy of Disliking Hillary Clinton." *Time*, March 15, 2016. https://time.com/4258976/disliking-hillary-clinton/.

Tannen, Deborah. *You Just Don't Understand: Women and Men in Conversation*. New York: Ballantine Books, 1990.

Tannen, Deborah. *You're the Only One I Can Tell*. New York: Ballantine Books, 2017.

Taub, Amanda. "Why Are Women-Led Nations Doing Better with Covid-19?" *New York Times*, May 15, 2020. https://www.nytimes.com/2020/05/15/world/coronavirus-women-leaders.html.

Tebbe, Don. *Chief Executive Transitions: How to Hire and Support a Nonprofit CEO*. Washington, D.C.: BoardSource, 2008.

Thompson, Johnny. "How 'Chesterton's Fence' Can Help You Avoid Terrible Decisions." Big Think, November 16, 2023. https://bigthink.com/business/chestertons-fence/.

Tillers, Saskia. "Why Women Like Jacinda Ardern Make Such Strong Leaders." *CEO Magazine*, November 4, 2020. https://www.theceomagazine.com/business/management-leadership/jacinda-ardern-strong-leader/.

Treviño, Veronica, Zannie Giraud Voss, Christine Anagnos, and Alison D. Wade. "The Ongoing Gender Gap in Art Museum Directorships." March 22, 2017. https://aamd.org/sites/default/files/document/AAMD%20NCAR%20Gender%20Gap%202017.pdf.

Tuitt, Franklin A., Mary Ann Danowitz Sagaria, and Caroline Sotello Viernes Turner. "Signals and Strategies in Hiring Faculty of Color." In *Higher Education: Handbook of Theory and Research*, edited by John C. Smart: 497–535. Vol. 22, 2007.

United States Census Bureau. "Older People Projected to Outnumber Children for First Time in U.S. History." Last modified October 8, 2019. https://www.census.gov/newsroom/press-releases/2018/cb18-41-population-projections.html.

United States Government Accountability Office. "Women in the Workforce: The Gender Pay Gap Is Greater for Certain Racial and Ethnic Groups and Varies by Education Level." Published December 15, 2022. https://www.gao.gov/products/gao-23-106041.

Valentine, Gerry. "Executive Presence: What Is It, Why You Need It and How to Get It." *Forbes*, July 31, 2018. https://www.forbes.com/sites/forbescoachescouncil/2018/07/31/executive-presence-what-is-it-why-you-need-it-and-how-to-get-it/?sh=5224ff246bc7.

Van Gennep, Arnold. *The Rites of Passage*. Translated by Monika B. Vizedom and Gabrielle L. Caffee. Chicago: University of Chicago Press, 2019.

Vuleta, Geoff. "Corner Office: Can You Handle the 100-Day To-Do List?" Interview by Adam Bryant, *New York Times*, November 20, 2010. https://www.nytimes.com/2010/11/21/business/21corner.html.

Wahlstrom, Jeff. "Succession Planning Should Not Be Confused with Funeral Planning." Starboard Leadership Consulting, LLC. Accessed February 23, 2024, https://www.starboardleadership.com/leadership-transitions/succession-planning-should-not-be-confused-with-funeral-planning/.

Washington, Ella. "Recognizing and Responding to Microaggressions at Work." *Harvard Business Review*, May 10, 2022. https://hbr.org/2022/05/recognizing-and-responding-to-microaggressions-at-work.

Watkins, Michael D. "How Managers Become Leaders." *Harvard Business Review*, June 2012. https://hbr.org/2012/06/how-managers-become-leaders.

Wilde, Tyler. "GDC 2013: BioWare's David Gaider Asks, 'How about we just decide how not to repel women?'" *PC Gamer*, March 29, 2013. https://www.pcgamer.com/bioware-david-gaider-sex-in-video-game/.

Wittenberg-Cox, Avivah. "Learn to Get Better at Transitions." *Harvard Business Review*, July 5, 2018. https://hbr.org/2018/07/learn-to-get-better-at-transitions.

Zernike, Kate. "The Campus Wars Aren't About Gender . . . Are They?" *New York Times*, January 28, 2024. https://www.nytimes.com/2024/01/28/us/colleges-antisemitism-gender.html.

Zheng, Wei, Ronit Kark, and Alyson Meister. "How Women Manage the Gendered Norms of Leadership." *Harvard Business Review*, November 28, 2018. https://hbr.org/2018/11/how-women-manage-the-gendered-norms-of-leadership.

Index

AAMD. *See* Association of Art
   Museum Directors
ABC Entertainment, 71
ABR mindset. *See* "always be
   recruiting" mindset
abundance mindset, 16–17
access, DEAI, 65, 95, 121
adaptability, xii, 48
advisors, 13, 15, 75–76, 78, 90,
   105–6, 111
agility, xi–xii, 51–52, 95
agility quotient. *See* AQ
AI. *See* artificial intelligence
"always be recruiting" (ABR)
   mindset, 4, 33–34
ambiguous. *See* VUCA
announcements, departures, 18–20
AnswerDash, 51
AQ (agility quotient), 51
Ardern, Jacinda, 47
Art and Healing exhibition (Mia),
   50–51
artificial intelligence (AI), 3, 28, 123
Association of Art Museum
   Directors (AAMD), 60, 137
The Atlantic (magazine), 49–50
Austin, A. Everett "Chick," 14–15
authenticity, 28, 46, 61, 78–79, 82
Autodesk, 73
"Axial Age," x

Baby Boomers (Gen X), 2, 3
Baker, David L., viii
Bartleby column (*The Economist*), 51

Bass, Carl, 73
behavior, 35, 65–67, 108
Bem Sex Role Inventory (BSRI), 62
Beshati, Naz, 111
Best Buy, 45, 82, 91
bias: behaviors to watch out for,
   65–67; communication and,
   63–64, 79; executive presence,
   59; gender, 58–59, 63–64, 79;
   with glass ceiling or labyrinth,
   60–61; with leadership difference
   and gender roles, 61–63;
   modern sexism, 59–60; racism,
   discrimination and, 57, 58,
   64–65; types of, 44–45, 57–59,
   64–67, 116
Bielińska, Inga, 59
Black, Indigenous, People of Color
   (BIPOC), 39, 65
Bloomberg, Michael, 49–50
Bloomberg Businessweek (journal),
   82
BLS. *See* Bureau of Labor Statistics
boards (trustees), 21, 50–51;
   directors and, 11–13, 15–16, 18, 38,
   109–11; dynamics with searches,
   24–25; first six months and
   role of, 83–84; first-time CEOs
   working with, 108–10; interim
   period tips for, 115–17; "10 Ways
   Boards Screw Up Leadership
   Transitions," 22, 30
Board Source, 1
body language, 20, 48, 80

Boston Museum of Fine Art, 17
Bradt, George B., 21, 34, 71–72, 74, 96, 108, 115
Braun, Lloyd, 71
Brown, Brené, 79
Bryant, Adam, 39, 98, 115
BSRI. *See* Bem Sex Role Inventory
Bureau of Labor Statistics (BLS), 13
Burkeman, Oliver, 16, 86
burning imperative, 91, 92
Burns, Robert, 47

candidates: CEO interview, 34–36; EI of, 48–49; "How to Evaluate a Job Candidate's Critical Thinking Skills in an Interview," 45; internal, 4, 26, 103–5; job offers, 39–40; "nontraditional," 66
career check-in, five-year: abundance or scarcity mindsets, 16–17; challenges to tackle, 15; circle of advisors, 15; feedback and criticism, 14; "going to the next level," 14; growth opportunities, 13–14, 16, 17; high-functioning leadership team, 14; relationship with board, 15–16; risk-taking for future growth, 13–14; sabbaticals, 17; strategies driven by public need, 14–15; work as energizing or debilitating, 15, 16
career switching, 2–3, 113
Carli, Linda L., 61
Carville, James, 4
Castile, Philando, 50
Castile, Valerie, 50
Census Bureau, US, 2
CEOs, 4, 6–7, 114–15; appointing internal, 104–5; candidate interview, 34–36; *Chief Executive Transitions*, 26; "disease," 46; first-time, 105–10; "The Mindsets and Practices of Excellent CEOs," 104; *The Secrets of Great CEO Selection*, 33; "Seven Surprises for New CEOs," 105. *See also* leadership; *specific CEOs*
The CEO Test (Bryant and Sharer), 115
Chait, Richard, 106
Chamorro-Premuzic, Tomas, 47
change management, 43, 51–52, 125
Charan, Ram, 30, 33, 37
Check, Jayme A., 34, 74, 96, 115
"Chesterton's Fence," 92
chicken truck plan, emergency, 6–7
Chief Executive Transitions (Tebbe), 26
Ciampa, Dan, viii, 74, 77, 86, 91
Citrin, James M., 99, 107
climate change, xi, xii, 3, 28
Clinton, Hillary, 58, 61
coalition building, 96
cocktail parties, 21, 23, 84
Cohn, Marc, viii
collaboration, 45, 49, 62, 96, 98–99, 108, 119
Collins, Jim, 44, 46, 90
committed stakeholders, 96
communication, 7, 18–19, 39, 43; executive presence and strong, 59; gender bias and, 63–64, 79; listening and, 45, 46, 48, 49, 79–81; nonverbal, 20, 48, 80; six to twelve months on job, 97–98
community, 23–24, 66, 96
compensation plan, 30–31
complex. *See* VUCA
confidentiality, 18, 23, 24, 25, 84, 104
confirmation bias, 45, 65
conflict management, 48
Congress, US, 60, 72
contributors, stakeholders, 96
The Corner Office (Bryant), 39
courage, xii, 43, 49–51, 116, 124–25
Covey, Stephen, ix, 16
COVID-19 pandemic, xii, 3, 47, 51, 62–63, 73, 122–23
creativity: interview questions, 125–26; *Liminal Creativity*, ix

credibility, personal, 77, 85–86
critical thinking, 43–45, 51–52, 64, 123
criticism, feedback and, 14
cultural competence, 29, 53, 65
culture, institutional, 52, 80, 83, 96, 97, 99
culture fit, interview questions, 122
"the Culture Web," 97
Cunff, Anne-Laure, ix
curiosity, 43–47, 50, 71, 123

Danowitz Sagaria, Mary Ann, 66
Dante Alighieri, vii, xii, 116–17
"dark side," of leaders, 48
Davey, Lian, 52
Dayton, Bruce B., 38
DEAI (diversity, equity, access and inclusion), 65, 95, 121
debilitating, work as, 15, 16
DEI (diversity, equity and inclusion), 43, 52–53
demographics, in US, 39
departure-defined succession planning, 7
departures, xi, 13–20
detractors, stakeholders, 96
development, 4–5, 99
Dewar, Carolyn, 104
DiAngelo, Robin, 64, 65
Digital Equipment Corporation, 2
directors, boards and, 11–13, 15–16, 18, 38, 109–11. See also leadership
disability, 57, 58
discrimination, 57–60, 64–65. See also bias
diversity, 24, 39, 43, 52–53, 65, 95, 121
The Divine Comedy (Dante), vii, xii, 116–17
double consciousness, 64
the double bind, 58–59, 65–66
Drucker, Peter, 75, 81, 97
Du Bois, W. E. B., 64
Dweck, Carol S., 45–46, 98–99

Eagly, Alice, 61
echo chambers, 15
Eckert, Robert, 80
The Economist (magazine), 43, 51
EI. See emotional intelligence
Eight Secrets to a (Fairly) Fulfilled Life column (Burkeman), 16
emergencies, chicken truck plan, 6–7
Emmerling, Robert, 48
Emotional Intelligence (Goleman), 47–48
emotional (quotient) intelligence (EI, EQ), 51; interview questions, 123–24; leadership and, 43, 44, 47–49
emotions, 14, 20, 115; fear, vii–viii, xi, 21–22, 45, 51–52, 73, 82, 113; nonverbal cues and, 80
empathy, 46, 48, 62, 63, 64, 95
employee assistance program hotline, 100
energizing, work as, 15, 16
environmental sustainability, interview questions, 121–22
EQ (emotional quotient). See emotional intelligence
Equal Justice Initiative, 15
equity: DEAI, 65, 95, 121; DEI, 43, 52–53
Eurich, Tasha, 48
executive presence, 59
external factors: searches, 28–29; selection process, 38–39

fear, vii–viii, xi, 21–22, 45, 51–52, 73, 82, 113
feedback, criticism and, 14
Feiler, Bruce, x–xi, 27, 73
Fels, Anna, 62
first hire, transition type, 26
first-time CEOs, 105–10
Five Rs, 3
"fixin' to" search phase, 25–27, 28–29, 33, 37
Forbes (magazine), xii, 59, 108

Fortune 500 companies, 60
Frank, Christopher, 45
Fuller, Joseph, 3
"the fuzzy front end," 74

Gallop, Cindy, 47
Garikipati, Supriya, 62–63
Garry, Joan, 22, 30
Garvan, David, 98
Gay, Claudine, 21
Geek Squad, 33–34
gender, 58–64, 79
generosity, 16, 62, 81, 95
genius, culture of, 99
Gen X (Baby Boomers), 2, 3
George, Bill, xii
Gerstner, Lou, 30
Gino, Francesca, 45
glass ceiling, labyrinth or, 60–61
"going to the next level," 14
Goldsmith, Marshall, 44, 75–76
Goleman, Daniel, 47–48
goodbye, long, xi
Good to Great (Collins), 44, 46,
    90
Google, 34
gravitas, 59, 65, 115
"the Great Resignation," 2–3
"growth identity," 14
growth opportunities, 13–14, 16, 17
The Guardian (newspaper), 16
GuideStar, 31
Gumz, Mark, 92
Guthrie, Tyrone, 83
Guthrie Theater, Minneapolis, 83

Haj, Joseph, 83
hard-to-follow executive, transition
    type, 26
Harman International, 98
Harvard Business Review (journal), 3,
    45, 98, 105
Harvard University, 21
Heen, Sheila, 14
Heidrick & Struggles, 106

Hewlett, Sylvia Ann, 59
hiring, search firm, 29–30
Hirt, Martin, 104
"How to Evaluate a Job Candidate's
    Critical Thinking Skills in an
    Interview" (Frank, Magnone and
    Netzer), 45
humility, 35, 37, 45–47, 50, 71, 82,
    106

IBM, 30
identity triggers, 14
Ideo, 45
imposter syndrome, 86
inclusion, 24, 43, 52–53, 65, 95, 121
The Inferno (Dante), 116–17
inspirational leadership, 48
integrity, 50, 95, 108
intelligence quotient. See IQ
internal candidates, 4, 26, 103–5
interview questions: change
    management, 125; courage,
    124–25; creativity/out-of-the-
    box thinking, 125–26; culture
    fit, 122; DEAI, 121; EI, 123–24;
    environmental sustainability,
    121–22; final, 126; general, 119;
    leadership, 120; management,
    119–20; as subset of three
    questions, 34; thoughts specific to
    organization, 122; values, 125
interviews: artificial environment of,
    34, 36, 49; candidates and job
    offers, 39–40; CEO candidate,
    34–36; committee, 34, 36–39;
    "How to Evaluate a Job
    Candidate's Critical Thinking
    Skills in an Interview," 45; STARR
    method with, 35
IQ (intelligence quotient), 47–48,
    51
Itzchakov, Guy, 80

James, William, x
Jaspers, Karl, x

job offers, factors to consider, 39–40.
    See also six months on the job; six
    to twelve months on the job
Johnson, Gerry, 97
Johnson, Steven, 99
Joly, Hubert, 45–46, 79, 82, 91

Kambhampati, Uma, 62–63
Keller, Scott, 51, 104
Kerr, William, 3
Khouri, Barbara, 48
Kimberly-Clark, 14
kindness, 62
Know Before You Go (Rorschach), 36
"know-it-all," "learn-it-all" versus, 45

labyrinth, glass ceiling or, 60–61
Lacy, Alan, 103
Lakoff, Robin, 58
lame duck, 3, 20, 74
Lawler, John A., 74, 96
leadership: agility, change
    management and, 51–52; CEOs,
    4, 6–7, 26, 33–36, 46, 104–10,
    114–15; courage and, 43, 49–51;
    critical thinking and, 43–45,
    51–52; curiosity and, 43, 45–47;
    "dark side" of, 48; deficit, 4; DEI
    and, 43, 52–53; directors, 11–13,
    15–16, 18, 38, 109–11; EI and,
    43, 44, 47–49; with executive
    presence, 59; five-year career
    check-in for, 13–17; gender roles
    and difference in, 61–63; humility
    and, 45–47, 82; interim, 6, 21–22;
    interview questions, 120; "Level
    5," 46; liminal stage of change
    in, x; mistakes, 76, 86; *The New
    Leader's 100-Day Action Plan*, 34,
    115; with predecessors, 85, 92;
    questions to staff from, 80–81;
    "seismic shifts" when moving into,
    106; "7 Leadership Lessons Men
    Can Learn from Women," 47;
    with "silent advisory board," 111;

succession planning for departure
    of, 2–4; team, 4, 6–7, 14, 39, 52,
    90–91, 107; "10 Ways Boards
    Screw Up Leadership Transitions,"
    22, 30; types and behavior, 108;
    volunteer, viii; "VUCA leaders,"
    xii; vulnerability and, 43, 79, 82,
    84; *Women and the Labyrinth of
    Leadership*, 61; of women with
    COVID-19, 47, 62–63. *See also* six
    months on the job; six to twelve
    months on the job
Leading the Fight Against Covid
    (Garikipati and Kambhampati),
    62–63
learning organization, modeling of,
    98–99
"learn-it-all," "know-it-all" versus, 45
legacy issues, resolving, 27–28
"letting go of what was," xi
"Level 5" leaders, 46
LGBTQI community, 60
Life Is in the Transitions (Feiler), x–xi,
    27
Liminal Creativity (Cunff), ix
liminality, ix–xi
listening, 45, 46, 48, 49, 79–81
Lopez, Ian Hany, 66
Lorsch, Jay W., 105

MacKay, Malcolm, 17
Magnone, Paul, 45
management, 1–2, 48; change, 43,
    51–52, 125; interview questions,
    119–20
map, of stakeholders, 78–79
Mattel, 80
Mayer, John, 47
McKinsey & Company, 78, 82
media, 7, 12, 18–19, 75, 78, 85, 122
Medtronic, xii
Mehrabian, Albert, 48
Memphis Brooks Museum of Art,
    vii, 2
men, 47, 57–64, 79, 107

messy middle, xi

metamessages, 63, 79

Mia. *See* Minneapolis Institute of Art

microaggressions, 64, 66

Microsoft, 45, 46

Millennials, 2

Mindset (Dweck), 45–46, 98–99

mindsets, 4–5, 16–17, 33–34, 45–46, 71, 98–99, 104

"The Mindsets and Practices of Excellent CEOs" (Dewar, Hirt and Keller), 104

Minneapolis Institute of Art (Mia), 38, 50–51

mission, with vision and values, 92–95, 97–98

mistakes: leadership, 76, 86; search committee, 44

modern sexism, 59–60

Ms. California competition, 60–61

Murphy, Kate, 79, 80

Muslims, 65

Nadella, Satya, 45, 46

National Gallery of Art, 60, 75, 78, 80, 83, 85–86, 93, 95

Neff, Thomas J., 99, 107

Netzer, Oded, 45

The New Leader's 100-Day Action Plan (Bradt, Check and Pedroza), 34, 115

New York Times (newspaper), 2, 17, 79

Niedenthal, Paula, 79

Nohria, Nitin, 105, 108

nondisclosure agreement, 25

Olsen, Ken, 2

Olympus Corporation, 92

one hundred days on the job, 72–73, 77–81. *See also* six months on the job

optimism, 16, 48, 72

organization: change management, 125; interview questions with thoughts specific to, 122

out-of-the-box thinking, interview questions, 125–26

"paint the lobby," 77–81, 95, 115

Paliwal, Dinesh, 98

"the paradox of success," 75–76

passion, patience and political savvy, 23

Pedroza, Jorge E., 34, 115

people of color, 39, 40, 50, 58, 64–67, 121

Pew Research, 3

plans: compensation, 30–31; culture, 97; emergency chicken truck, 6–7; for first six months on the job, 81–83, 84; *The New Leader's 100-Day Action Plan*, 34, 115; for six to twelve months on job, 91–92. *See also* succession planning

Pliner, Eric, 91

political savvy, 23, 59

Porray, Mary Elizabeth, 78

Porter, Michael E., 105

predecessors, leadership with, 85, 92

preparation: for new leadership role, 74–75; search, 25–27

press releases, departures, 18–19

privilege, bias and, 57

public need, strategies driven by, 14–15

questions: interview, 34, 119–26; from leadership to staff, 80–81

racial bias, 66

racism, 57, 58, 64–65

reconsideration (work-life balance), 3

recruitment, ABR mindset, 4, 33–34

rejection, 35

relationship management, EI and, 48

relationship triggers, 14

relocation, 3, 73, 114

reluctance (to return to in-person jobs), 3

reshuffling, 3
responsiveness, agility and, 95
résumés, whitening, 58, 66
retirement, 2, 3, 7, 11, 22
review process, CEO, 4
Reynolds, Russell, 4
RHR International, 107
Right from the Start (Ciampa and
    Watkins), viii, 77, 91
"the right appearance," executive
    presence with, 59
risks: future growth with, 13–14,
    113–14; six months on the job,
    86
rites, liminal, x
The Rites of Passage (Van Gannep), x
Roosevelt, Franklin Delano, 72, 83
Rorschach, Kimerly, 36
Rost, Joseph, 62
Ryan, William, 106

sabbaticals, 17
salaries: compensation plan, 30–31;
    for interim leadership, 22; for
    women and people of color, 40
Salavoy, Peter, 47
"savior thinking," 28
scarcity mindset, 16–17
Schmidt, Eric, 34
Scholes, Kevan, 97
search committees: assembling,
    22–24; with EI of candidates,
    48–49; ideal size, 23; mistakes,
    44; transitions and, xi–xii, 116
search firms, 25, 29–30
the search: assembling committee
    for, 22–24; compensation plan,
    30–31; confidentiality, 18, 23, 24,
    25; external factors, 28–29; "fixin'
    to" phase, 25–27, 28–29, 33, 37;
    global studies on, 106; hiring firms
    for, 29–30; interim leadership, 21–
    22; internal candidates, 26, 103–4;
    legacy issues to resolve, 27–28;
    preparing for, 25–27; thinking

ahead, 27; trustee dynamics,
    24–25
Sears, 103
Seattle Art Museum, 36
The Secrets of Great CEO Selection
    (Charan), 33
the selection: with ABR mindset,
    33–34; candidates and job offers,
    39–40; CEO candidate interview,
    34–36; external factors, 38–39;
    interview committee, 34, 36–39;
    The Secrets of Great CEO Selection,
    33
self-awareness, vii, 17, 48–49, 106
self-evaluation, 4
self-management, EI and, 48
self-reflection, xii, 75–77
Sensoy, Özlem, 64, 65
Seppala, Emma, 79
"7 Leadership Lessons Men Can
    Learn from Women" (Chamorro-
    Premuzic and Gallop), 47
"Seven Surprises for New CEOs"
    (Porter, Lorsch and Nohria), 105
*The Seven Habits of Highly Successful
    People* (Covey), 16
sexism, 57–60, 107
Sharer, Kevin, 98, 115
"shift response," 79
"silent advisory board," 111
six months on the job: first one
    hundred days, 77–81; getting
    started, 71–72; obsession with
    first one-hundred days, 72–73;
    personal credibility, 77, 85–86;
    plan for, 81–83, 84; predecessor,
    85; preparing for new role, 74–75;
    prior to arrival, 73; risks, 86; role
    of board, 83–84; self-reflection,
    75–77
six to twelve months on the
    job: being tested, 99–100;
    "Chesterton's Fence," 92; coalition
    building, 96; communication,
    97–98; culture, 97; with learning

organization modeled, 98–99; mission, vision and values, 92–95; plan refinement for strategic framework, 91–92; strategic framework, 91–92, 95–96; taking stands, 100; talent building, 90–91; vision, 89–90

skills: critical thinking, 43–45, 51–52, 64, 123; "soft," 5, 43, 46–47; technical, 44

Smith, Darwin, 14

social awareness, EI and, 48

social media, 75, 85, 122

Society for Human Resource Management, 1–2

"soft skills," 5, 43, 46–47

"soft starts," 76

"solution selling," 34

staff: announcing departures to, 19–20; employee assistance program hotline, 100; high-functioning, 26; with internal CEO appointments, 104–5; questions from leadership to, 80–81; search committees and, 24; talent building, 90–91

stakeholders, 78–79, 96

stand, taking a, 100

Stanford Social Innovation Review, 2, 4

STARR method, with interviews, 35

Star Trek mission and vision, 94

Stephens, Robert, 33–34

Stevenson, Bryan, 15

Stone, Douglas, 14

strategic framework, 91–92, 95–96

strategies, public need driving, 14–15

strengths, weaknesses, opportunities and threats (SWOT), 27

success, 26, 45–46, 71–72, 75–76, 98–99

succession planning, 13, 21, 114; components, 5–7; departure-defined, 7; for departure of leaders, 2–4; reasons for, 1–2; short-term issues, 7; as talent

assessment and development strategy, 4–5; topics, 8

sustained success, transition type, 26

Swatch, 48

SWOT. *See* strengths, weaknesses, opportunities and threats

takeoff and landing, viii, 20, 74

talent, 4–5, 90–91

Tannen, Deborah, 58, 61, 63, 65–66, 79

Taylor, Barbara, 106

team, leadership, 4, 6–7, 14, 39, 52, 90–91, 107

teamwork, 48, 91

Tebbe, Don, 26, 28

technical skills, 44

Teitelbaum, Matthew, 17

"10 Ways Boards Screw Up Leadership Transitions" (Garry), 22, 30

tenures, average, viii, 11, 13

tested, being, 99–100

Thanks for the Feedback (Stone and Heen), 14

"threshold competence," 48

Time magazine, 65–66

To a Louse (Burns), 47

traditional sexism, 60

training, leadership, 107

transformative change, 52

transitions: *Chief Executive Transitions*, 26; emotions with, vii–viii, xi, 21–22, 51–52, 73, 82, 113, 115; *Life Is in the Transitions*, x–xi, 27; liminality, ix–xi; roadblocks, viii–ix; search committees and, xi–xii, 116; "seismic shifts" with leadership, 106; "10 Ways Boards Screw Up Leadership Transitions," 22, 30. *See also* departures; six months on the job; six to twelve months on the job

triggers, feedback, 14

"troubles talk," 63

trustees. *See* boards
truth triggers, 14
turnaround, transition type, 26
Turner, Victor (1920-1983), x

uncertain. *See* VUCA
underperforming, transition type, 26
understanding. *See* "VUCA leaders"
United States (US), 2, 39, 60, 72
US Army War College, xi

Valentine, Gerry, 59
values: institutional, xii, 50, 94-95,
    123; interview questions, 125;
    mission, vision and, 92-95, 97-98
values statement, 27, 93, 94
Van Gannep, Arnold (1873-1957), ix-x
Virgil, 113, 116-17
vision, 77-78, 89-90, 92-95, 97-98
"Vision, Understanding, Courage,
    Adaptability leaders." *See* "VUCA
    leaders"
Volatile, Uncertain, Complex,
    Ambiguous. *See* VUCA
volunteers, viii, 7, 23, 25-26, 30, 116
VUCA (Volatile, Uncertain, Complex,
    Ambiguous), xi-xii, 51, 94
"VUCA (Vision, Understanding,
    Courage, Adaptability) leaders," xii

Vuleta, Geoff, 97
vulnerability, ix, 43, 63, 79, 82, 84

Wadsworth Athenaeum, 14
Wahlstrom, Jeff, 1
"Walking in Memphis," viii
watchers, stakeholders, 96
Watkins, Michael, viii, 74, 77, 86, 91,
    106
*What Got You Here Won't Get You
    There* (Goldsmith), 44, 75-76
Where Good Ideas Come From
    (Johnson, S.), 99
whitening résumés, 58, 66
Wittenberg-Cox, Avivah, xi
Wobbrock, Jake, 51
women, 40, 46-47, 57-66, 79, 107
*Women and the Labyrinth of
    Leadership* (Eagly and Carli), 61
work-life balance (reconsideration),
    3
A World of Pure Experience (James), x
World War II, 83

You Just Don't Understand (Tannen),
    63
You're in Charge, Now What? (Neff
    and Citrin), 99, 107
You're Not Listening (Murphy), 79

About the Author

Kaywin Feldman is the director of the National Gallery of Art in Washington, D.C. She was appointed in 2019, the first woman to lead the nation's art museum. As director, Feldman is committed to connecting people to art in a globalized world through the power of wonder and accessibility. Before joining the National Gallery, she served as Nivin and Duncan MacMillan director and president at the Minneapolis Institute of Art (Mia) from 2008 to 2019 and led the Memphis Brooks Museum of Art from 1999 to 2007.

Feldman is a member of the board of directors of the Terra Foundation for American Art and a trustee of the National Trust for Historic Preservation and the White House Historical Association. She is a past president of the Association of Art Museum Directors (AAMD) and past chair of the American Alliance of Museums (AAM). Feldman received an MA in art history from the Courtauld Institute of Art, University of London; an MA in museum studies from the Institute of Archaeology at the University of London; and a BA, summa cum laude, in classical archaeology from the University of Michigan. She lectures and publishes widely on museums in the twenty-first century.